D0597722

POISON FARM
A MURDERER UNMASKED
AFTER 60 YEARS

David Williams

THOROGOOD

Published by Thorogood Publishing Ltd April 2004
Reprinted May 2004

Thorogood Publishing Ltd
10-12 Rivington Street London EC2A 3DU
Telephone: 020 7749 4748 • Fax: 020 7729 6110
Email: info@thorogood.ws • Web: www.thorogood.ws

A CIP catalogue record for this book is available
from the British Library.

ISBN 1 85418 259 5

Cover and Book designed by Driftdesign

Printed in Great Britain by Ashford Colour Press

Dedication

To Syd and Rose Williams and their many progeny.

Acknowledgements

My thanks are particularly due to my daughter Susie, who guided me through the workings of the Public Records Office and the Probate Search Room, to our local historian Clive Paine, who advised me on historical accuracy about West Suffolk in the late 1930s, to my wife Elizabeth, who read the text (several times) and made many useful amendments and suggestions, and to my son John for his digital magic on the illustrations.

David Williams

The author

David Williams was born in Risby, scene of the Murfitt murder. He joined his local weekly paper, the Bury Free Press, in Bury St Edmunds as a trainee reporter and worked on a variety of provincial papers before joining the Daily Mirror in 1955. After ten years he left Fleet Street in 1965, becoming editor of the South East London Mercury, then editor of the Evening Echo in Southend, where he met his wife Elizabeth.

He became editor of the Evening Argus in Brighton in 1978 and it was there he was named the country's Journalist of the Year in the 1984 British Press Awards for his paper's coverage of the Grand Hotel bombing and his personal reporting of the Ethiopian famine.

In 1985 he returned to Fleet Street as deputy editor of The People and later Robert Maxwell's planning group. But sensing all was not well with the company and its flamboyant proprietor he found a happy way out – back to Bury St Edmunds as editor of his first paper, the Bury Free Press, until he retired in 1997.

He was national president of the Guild of Editors, a member of the Press Complaints Commission and was made an MBE for services to journalism.

Contents

Main characters

BILL MURFITT

Buccaneering farmer who, after an adventurous early life, settles down at Quays Farm in the Suffolk village of Risby. He works hard, plays hard and has an eye for the ladies. His sudden death shocks the village and leads to a murder hunt.

GERTRUDE MURFITT

Bill's quiet, devoted wife and mother to their two sons, Leslie and Billy. She is tortured by her husband's affair but stays with him. She has a motive for murder and is a prime suspect.

CHARLIE AND ELAINE BROWNE

The Murfitt's best friends who farm in the next village. The families share a secret shame which also brings the Browne's under suspicion by Scotland Yard detectives.

JAMES WALKER

Describes himself as a gentleman farmer, lives at Hall Farm, half a mile from the Murfitts. After his wife's death he employs a housekeeper and they build up a close relationship. His vacillation while being questioned brings him under suspicion.

MARY CHANDLER

She is also known as Fernie Chandler. Walker's Scottish-born housekeeper who has a troubled past and strange habits. She is facing a court case accused of theft and Bill Murfitt's evidence is vital to the case. Another suspect.

DETECTIVE CHIEF INSPECTOR LEONARD BURT

Country-born and one of Scotland Yard's rising stars. His quiet, persistent methods have already sent killers to the gallows but the Murfitt case is his biggest challenge so far. He is destined for the top.

DETECTIVE SERGEANT REGINALD SPOONER

Burt's Cockney assistant who doesn't like life in the country. He's known for his aggressiveness in questioning but he has a high reputation for getting evidence that matters. He is also destined for the top in Scotland Yard.

Risby in 1938

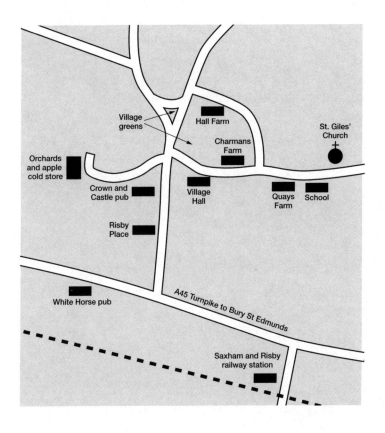

Village greens

Hall Farm

St. Giles' Church

Charmans Farm

Orchards and apple cold store

Crown and Castle pub

Village Hall

Quays Farm

School

Risby Place

A45 Turnpike to Bury St Edmunds

White Horse pub

Saxham and Risby railway station

One Cyanide in the salts

One
Cyanide in the salts

As I sat in the ordered quiet of the reading room I wondered what the file on the table in front of me would tell me about William Murfitt. It was a question that had been with me since that day more than 60 years ago when my father, his face covered in worry, came home unexpectedly in mid-morning and told my mother, 'The boss is dead'.

I was coming up for six at the time and off from school with a cold. My mother told me to go and play in the front room while she made a cup of tea. I heard them talking in undertones, disbelief in their voices, anxiety in their tone. My father was Murfitt's foreman and his sudden death made them worry about the future, particularly whether Dad's job would still be safe. In the following weeks it seemed as though the farmer's death was the only subject of conversation for our family and everyone else we knew. With the other children in the village I watched excitedly as policemen searched barns and ditches, as reporters and photographers knocked on people's doors and gathered outside the village pub, always asking questions about my Dad's boss.

Those memories, still crystal clear, were perhaps the first full ones in my life. Now, as I sat in the Public Record Office with the large cardboard folder bulging with papers in front of me, I skimmed through the pages. I had feared that the file might be just a few cuttings and some sparse notes written in frustration by the two Scotland Yard detectives who came to our village to search for a poisoner and failed. Instead there was a long and detailed report of some 40,000 words containing vital evidence which could not be revealed at the time. As I turned the last few pages I knew that at last I had the answer to the mystery that remained when the detectives and the reporters left our village in the autumn of 1938. I now knew who murdered William Murfitt.

• •

BILL MURFITT HAD WOKEN UP at 5.30am in his Tudor farmhouse at Quays Farm in the quiet, ancient Suffolk village of Risby just outside Bury St Edmunds. The air was still moist from overnight rain, something he welcomed because there had been little in the previous few weeks and the drought was affecting the spring crops. In the farmyard he eased his 17-stone bulk into his Ford Eight, leaving his favourite car, the bulbous black American Buick, parked beside the barn and drove off into the village and to his fields just beyond. Everything looked and smelled fresher than it had done for a long time and the prospects for the summer were good. Later, back at the farm, he went about the normal business of the day, discussing the coming day's work with his foreman Syd Williams, working in his outside office until going into the house for breakfast just before 8.30. His wife Gertrude was in the dining room with his secretary Mollie Targett, who lived in during the week. As she did every morning Gertrude went to the sideboard and picked up a tin of Fynnon Salts, put a teaspoonful of the white powder in a glass and poured in hot water from a jug before putting the glass down in Bill's place.

'Aren't you having any salts this morning?' Murfitt asked his wife. 'No, I just don't fancy any today,' she replied.

Gertrude Murfitt, William Murfitt's wife

William Murfitt

Murfitt picked up the glass, took a large swig and immediately pulled a face. 'These taste a bit nasty, are you sure you didn't give me your dose as well?' he asked. She assured him it was the usual dose. A minute or so later he got up, clutched at his stomach and gasped, 'My God Gertie! I've got a terrible pain, I feel really ill. Get the doctor.' With that he stumbled round the table, his face reddening by the second, and slumped into another chair, from which he fell with a thud on to the polished wooden floor. At 8.30 am on Tuesday, May 17, 1938, after 56 years of life always active but not always good, Bill Murfitt lay dying in front of the wife he had both loved and cheated on, his face contorted from pain and fear, feeling as if a thousand devils were trying to tear his body apart.

• •

Doctor Hubert Ware was getting ready for morning surgery in Bury St Edmunds when the telephone rang. It was Mollie Target, asking him to go out to Risby immediately as her boss had been taken very ill. He picked up his bag and as he drove the four miles to Risby he checked in his mind what he knew about Murfitt... very active... diabetes... overweight. But he knew his patient had lately been sticking to his diet and he had seen him only a month ago, when there was no sign of impending trouble. At the farmhouse Dr Ware saw Murfitt on the floor, propped up by cushions under his back, where he had been left by two farmhands who had come running in after a maid called to them for help. He was still breathing but unconscious, his face still red, his eyes staring and his body trembling. Then, 40 minutes after taking the salts, Murfitt emitted a last throaty gurgle and died.

Dr Ware broke the news to Mrs Murfitt, who at first appeared quite calm. She handed him the tin of Fynnon Salts and pointed out that the salts and the paper in which they were contained were brownish in colour. Ware smelt the salts. 'Bitter almonds,' he said, and he was immediately suspicious. He was a keen gardener and always associated that smell with potassium cyanide which was used widely to destroy wasps' and hornets' nests. He asked if he could use the telephone and dialled the police station in Bury.

The Murfitt's housemaid Doris Howard looked out and saw Syd Williams in the farmyard as he returned from breakfast. She called out to him and as he came to the door she asked him to help lift Murfitt's body on to a camp bed. As he half carried and half pulled his boss's body across the dining room floor the foreman, who had become well acquainted with death in the horror of the trenches at Ypres, knew the worst had happened.

The first policeman to arrive was Constable Ernest Carrington, who had cycled from his house two miles away after a call from Bury St Edmunds police station. He was joined soon afterwards by his sergeant, Clifford Bigmore, who supervised the district covering Risby and other villages to the west of Bury. He went in and saw Murfitt's body on the camp bed. By now Mrs Murfitt was crying and almost hysterical. 'I wish I had taken a dose as well,' she called out. The sergeant told PC Carrington to arrange to have the body removed to the West Suffolk Hospital in Bury.

As Sergeant Bigmore looked around the dining room it occurred to him that for a room where a man had collapsed and died in agony while at breakfast it was very neat and tidy.

There was no cloth or dishes on the table, only a tumbler containing clear liquid and a spoon covered in a white powder. All the chairs were arranged neatly round the table. He asked Mrs Murfitt if anything had been moved since her husband died.

Mrs Murfitt, still in a state of hysteria, told him rather huffily that she had asked the maids to tidy up the room before the doctor arrived. The sergeant was kind and tried to placate her, but he knew it was a question that would have to be raised later because there had been interference with some of the evidence. He locked the door to the dining room with Murfitt's body still inside it and began to interview the staff. His task was not easy because Mrs Murfitt was still hysterical and crying and the maids kept going off to try to calm her down.

Sergeant Bigmore was joined soon afterwards by Sergeant George Willis, one of the West Suffolk force's only two detectives, and they began taking statements from the domestic staff and from friends and relatives of the Murfitt family who arrived after hearing of his death. The police enquiries went on for the rest of the day.

A hearse arrived at Quays Farm and Murfitt's body was taken to the West Suffolk General Hospital in Bury St Edmunds where that afternoon Dr Ware carried out a post mortem examination. He took out the stomach and carefully extracted the contents before putting the lot into two jars. Then he took out the kidneys and the liver and put them into separate jars. He sealed the jars and handed them to Detective Sergeant Willis who was waiting to take them to London for analysis. The room reeked of the stench of human remains combined with the bitter smell of cyanide.

It was a smell that was also well-known to Humphrey Walrond, Deputy Coroner for Bury St Edmunds, and he recognised it at once when a policeman walked into his office in Guildhall Street carrying a brown paper bag from which he took a tin of Fynnon Salts. He opened the tin and sniffed and was the second person that day to associate the acrid smell with wasps' nests. He returned the tin to the policeman and asked him to have the salts analysed and then began to write some notes on Murfitt's death to leave for the Coroner, Thomas Wilson, who was his brother-in-law. It was going to be an interesting case, from what he had heard of it so far.

Later that evening Humphrey Walrond drove the seven miles home to the village of Shimpling, where he found his wife in bed, looking tired but happy. As he walked into the bedroom he was already speaking, 'Something very exciting happened to me today, dear...' he began. Before he could explain further his wife smiled and said, 'You're not the only one, my darling, something very exciting happened to me as well.' And from the bedclothes she lifted up the baby son she had given birth to earlier that day at her parents' home a short distance away while her husband was confined to his office awaiting developments over Murfitt's death.

Walrond picked up his son, feeling guilty because he had not been at the house when he was born but exhilarated at the thought of being a father for the second time. What a day, he thought, one man dead and a new life born. That was how life went on.

Two **The murder hunt begins**

Two
The murder hunt begins

I shall never know whether the intense Press interest in our village after Murfitt's death subconsciously influenced my later choice of career but by the time I reached my early teens the only job I wanted was that of a reporter. On leaving school I was lucky enough to get a job on our local weekly, the Bury Free Press, and I spent the next 48 years in journalism, in the provinces and in Fleet Street, on newspapers good and bad. But it was not until I retired in the late 1990's that I was able to start fully researching the story I had grown up with as a boy and on which I had now collected a large file of newspaper cuttings as well as reminiscences and anecdotes related to me over the years by my father and other people in the village.

By placing letters in newspapers in East Anglia I contacted surviving members of Bill Murfitt's family who had their own collection of cuttings and memories, and I was able to build up a picture of the life and times of the farmer and the murder mystery that pushed our village on to the front pages of the nation's newspapers in that last full summer of peace before World War II.

IN THE MAY OF 1938 Captain Colin Robertson, Chief Constable of West Suffolk, was still getting to grips with the job he had taken over only in January. His main problem until now had been to ensure his police force was put on a war footing with the appointment of Air Raid Precaution wardens and special constables, as directed by the Home Office, as the news from Europe became worse. Robertson, wounded three times while serving in the Royal Artillery during World War I, was saddened by what he thought was the general acceptance throughout the country that there would soon be another conflict. He had been surprised, and inwardly pleased, to note that when Oswald Mosely brought his fascist Blackshirts to a market town like Bury St Edmunds for a weekend rally that a crowd of young men, many of them from the town's leading business families, had gone along to heckle the speakers and the meeting broke up in confusion. They were the same young men who were swelling the ranks of the Territorial Army at Gibraltar Barracks on the edge of the town and who were now training at weekends and summer camps with the Suffolk Regiment. He knew that if war did come he would inevitably be recalled to the colours because there were not many officers of his rank with experience of active service who had survived.

Robertson's deputy, Superintendent Archie Brinkley, had told him of the circumstances of Murfitt's death as soon as he received a report on Tuesday from Detective Sergeant Willis, and Robertson knew then that he could be facing his biggest challenge since joining the police force. Like many other chief constables at the time, he was a career soldier who had felt he could use his Army talents of organisation and discipline helping to secure law and order in peacetime. His previous post had been in charge of 70 policemen as Chief Constable of the Isle of Wight, where, it seemed to him, the most demanding job had been controlling the traffic during the island's increasingly busy holiday seasons. West Suffolk, with 170 policemen, was much busier but the crimes were still mainly of a minor nature. Now he had one to deal with, one which, on the first evidence, could well be murder.

On Wednesday, the day after Murfitt's death, Robertson asked Brinkley to set up a meeting with the two sergeants, George Willis the detective and Clifford Bigmore, in charge of the uniformed village constables on the west side of the town. The four of them met in Robertson's office near the Shire Hall, about a mile away from the main Bury St Edmunds police station.

Bigmore reported on what he found immediately on arriving at Quays Farm, commenting particularly on the fact that Mrs Murfitt seemed to have been almost over-keen on tidying up the dining room before the doctor or anyone else arrived. He also reported how he had asked the secretary, Mollie Targett, about the way Mrs Murfitt had served up the salts to her husband.

In the first place, it looked suspicious because the secretary said that normally Murfitt and his wife both took their salts before breakfast while yesterday she prepared a glass only for him. Mrs Murfitt had remarked to Miss Targett that the salts seemed a little damp and were brownish in colour, like a shade of brown sugar.

Mrs Murfitt mentioned the colouring to the secretary and then removed some of the brownish salts and some of the white ones with a teaspoon, putting them in a slop basin on the table. Miss Targett also said that after Murfitt drank from the glass his wife took the paper bag containing the salts from the tin and put them in the oven to dry because they seemed a little damp.

There were obviously questions to be asked about why Mrs Murfitt did not warn her husband there was something different about the salts that morning. On the other hand, if she had wanted to poison him without being suspected, why did she draw his secretary's attention to the salts in the first place? At an early stage in their discussions the police officers ruled out suicide. If Murfitt had wanted to poison himself it was hardly likely he would have gone to the lengths of allowing his wife to serve him the cyanide in a glass. So, if Mrs Murfitt was the poisoner, why had she done it? The four policemen discussed rumours that were already coming to light that Bill Murfitt was something of a ladies' man and had affairs behind his wife's back. There was no concrete evidence, but they put it down for further investigation. Then there was the case they were working on, dating back to the previous September, of a fur coat which disappeared from the home of a leading Newmarket trainer. The coat had been traced to Mrs Mary Chandler, housekeeper to another farmer in Risby, who had told police she bought the coat innocently from a woman she met at Newmarket races, which Mrs Chandler was attending with Murfitt. Murfitt had made a statement to the police about the matter and, although it seemed a tenuous link, the Chief Constable knew he would have to have it looked into. The policemen then discussed the options open to them. They had little experience of murder investigations, particularly as complicated as this might turn out to be. Also, apart from Sergeant Willis, the West Suffolk force had only one other detective, Constable Clem Fuller, who was at present on a course in Yorkshire. Robertson decided he had no other choice than to call for the help of Scotland Yard's Murder Squad and he made arrangements to travel to London the next day to arrange it.

• •

That evening, just after five o'clock, the landlord of the White Horse Inn, on the A45 halfway between Risby and the neighbouring village of Saxham, opened the door of his lounge bar to let in PC Carrington. The landlord had received a telephone call earlier in the day asking if he had a room which could be used for an inquest. He was told it would start at 6 o'clock and would be well over before his opening time of seven – which he thought was for the best, because you could hear what was going on in the lounge from the adjoining bar and he knew that some of his early-evening regulars would be curious to learn of anything which they might add to the stream of gossip already doing the rounds.

The lounge bar, with its wickerwork chairs, glass-topped tables and soft lighting, gave it an air of luxury which was appreciated by the racing crowd who found it a convenient stop on the way to and from Newmarket about ten miles away. Murfitt had been a regular there. The landlord and the policeman busied themselves setting out a couple of tables, with some chairs at the side for a jury, and other chairs in front for witnesses, police and the local Press who had been informed of the hearing.

Just before six o'clock Thomas Wilson, Coroner for the Liberty of Bury St Edmunds, walked into the room, shoulders erect, piercing eyes behind his spectacles, neat moustache. When everyone was seated the Coroner explained to the hastily-assembled jury that tonight's proceedings would be short, but they were necessary so that the deceased could be formally identified and that arrangements for the funeral could go ahead. He said a post mortem examination had been made but he was not in a position to lay before them a report on the result. When he asked who would give evidence of identification a stocky, ruddy-faced man in a well-cut suit stepped forward and announced himself as Rippon Charles Browne, farmer, from the neighbouring village of Fornham All Saints, a friend of the family. He took the oath and testified that he had seen the body of William Murfitt at approximately ten o'clock the day before at Quays Farm shortly after he had been pronounced dead by Dr Ware. He knew the deceased well and he and his wife and their young son had been guests of Mr and Mrs Murfitt on board their houseboat on the Norfolk Broads on Sunday, two days before Murfitt's death.

The Coroner, turning to the jury, warned them, 'When the inquest is resumed we shall have to hold it earlier in the day than this because it is obviously something which will take a little time.'

The investigation was formally underway, but at that stage neither the Coroner, nor anyone else, knew just how much time that would take, nor what extraordinary things would be uncovered about the life of William Murfitt, his family, his friends and his enemies in the process.

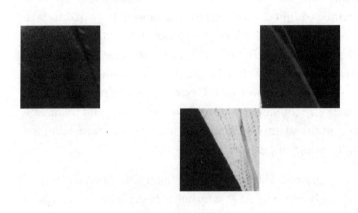

Three **Adventurer who settled down**

Three
Adventurer who settled down

THERE WAS NEVER A CHANCE that Bill Murfitt could ever have been slim, born as he was with an uncle like Samuel Murfitt who claimed to be The Largest Man in the World. Samuel was known as the Fat Man of Manea, the Fenland village where he lived and where his 40-stone body, complete with a 100-inch waist and a calf of 28 inches round, lasted until he was 54 and then gave up under the strain. He and his four brothers together weighed a ton and for his funeral they had to take a couple of rows of bricks from around the parlour window to get the coffin out. Bill Murfitt kept a newspaper cutting telling of his uncle's heavyweight fame at the back of the family album, but when anyone noticed it Gertrude always said it was just someone of the same name and nothing to do with them. She thought that if anyone found out there was a connection the family would appear common.

As a young man Bill was sturdy of build and showed a natural skill as a horseman. At first he helped out on his father's farm in the market town of March but at the age of 16, bored with life in the Fens, he went off to join the Cavalry. Because of his physique and horsemanship they believed him when he said he was 17 and let him enlist, and he soon found himself in the thick of the Boer War as one of the youngest sergeants in the British Army.

When the war ended in 1902 he returned to the Fens, aged just 20. Now a handsome, strapping young man bronzed by the South African sun, he made many a girl's heart flutter, none more so than Gertrude, one of three daughters of a publican in Chatteris, and they married in 1903. Their first son Leslie was born soon afterwards but it was not long before Bill was again looking for more excitement than the farm could offer. Leaving Gertrude at home to look after their son, he and a pal took up a couple of contracts looking after groups of around 20 horses which were being exported by sea from Europe to Japan. After the last trip he travelled on to Australia, where one of his jobs was to guard a fence running north to south through the Outback to stop the spread of rabbits. When home beckoned he didn't do it the easy way. He took a job on a tramp steamer and sailed back to England by way of Cape Horn.

He was now ready to settle down to farming and family life and their second son Billy was born in 1913. Finding there was a growing demand for carrots in London, Bill Murfitt put himself one move ahead of his competitors by building a washing plant to remove the black Fenland mud from the crop so that they reached Covent Garden ready for the pot. For a time the Murfitts lived in a big house he bought in the centre of the Cambridgeshire market town of Wisbech. Gertrude liked it because she thought its large rooms, huge garden and billiards room gave them a lift up the social scale. Bill, always the entrepreneur, hatched out chicks in incubators in the cellar and sold them on.

Later on Murfitt found carrots would grow better in the lighter land around King's Lynn so he took his family to Norfolk, where he pioneered the idea of contract farming. This meant he provided the seeds, fertilizer and the labour and other farmers provided their land and horses. Murfitt received a fixed fee for his work without having to finance a farm and the farmers benefited from the sale of the superior carrots he grew. He was one of the first to transport crops from the farm by road direct to Covent Garden, at one time using a steam-driven lorry that, even taking two days for the return journey, was still faster than using the railway.

By this time the young Murfitt family was growing up. Leslie was apprenticed at the rapidly expanding Vauxhall motor factory and went on to start his own business while Billy had joined his father on the farm. The number of photographs in the family album was growing, many of them of the Murfitt family relaxing at their beach hut at Hunstanton, where they went nearly every summer weekend. Others showed the family house, inevitably with two or three fast and interesting cars parked outside.

In contrast to the improving fortune of the Murfitt family, other farmers in East Anglia were experiencing hard times in the depression of the 20s and 30s. Many farms were left derelict, others sold off cheaply. Rents for those who wanted to become tenant farmers were low but few could find the capital to risk in equipping and running a farm in a declining economy.

It was in 1931 that Murfitt heard that the lease of Quays Farm in Risby was on the market. He drove down with Gertrude along the flat, black, Fenland roads into the lush and gradual undulating countryside of West Suffolk and they both immediately fell in love with the farmhouse, with its thirteen rooms providing plenty of space for family and visitors, as well as accommodation for servants on the top floor. The garden, which ran to one side of the house shielded from the road by a flint wall and dominated by a graceful fir tree, was a delight. But it was when they drove along the lanes that bordered the fields that he really decided this was the farm he wanted. The 500 acres immediately surrounding the farmhouse was loamy soil, not too heavy, and was ideal for the market garden type of crops, such as peas, beans, sprouts and cabbages, for which he knew there was a ready and quick market in London hotels. Further out, at Heath Barn on the edge of the village, was another 400 or more acres of light, sandy soil which had been converted from heathland and was not really suitable for the traditional Suffolk crops of cereals and sugar beet. Murfitt, however, knew it was ideal for his favourite crop, carrots, and he also wanted to grow more onions which he thought would do well there.

They met the agent of Sir John Wood, the baronet who lived in the neighbouring village at Hengrave Hall and who owned most of the land in Risby, and struck a deal – £5 an acre for the land in the village while the difficult land around Heath Barn would be rent-free for the first six months and £1 an acre after that. One thought in Gertrude's mind as they drove back to Norfolk might have been that Quays Farm would take up all Bill's time, and hopefully keep him out of mischief in other directions.

When they moved to Risby Murfitt's industry and his forward-looking approach to farming began to pay off immediately. He bought his first tractor at a time when many other farmers were still relying solely on horses and gradually his fleet grew to five, including two large tracked crawlers which pulled the first five-furrow plough to be seen in the county. He bought two Bedford Carrimore lorries so that young Billy and other drivers could take the crops direct to Covent Garden. On the way back they would call in at the London Docks to pick up fertiliser, seeds or corn for other farmers in the area who were happy to pay for the convenience. At one point, to save drivers being 24 hours at the wheel, Murfitt rented a room in a house in Epping Forest so that after a journey from Suffolk, one driver could be dropped off to sleep the night while another took the lorry on to London before returning to Epping. There the first driver would take over and drive back to Risby.

The harvesting of crops like peas and beans needed a lot of workers over a short period and Murfitt solved this problem by finding his own casual labour. When his lorries drove back to Risby through London's East End they would pick up unemployed men who were only to glad to be offered work. He found other casual labourers by sending a lorry to the Bury St Edmunds workhouse when they were turning out men in the mornings, and offering them a job. At pea-picking time, for example, they earned a shilling a bag and many of them would work until dark, sleep under the hedge and be back at work at daybreak to earn more money than they had ever done before. At any one time there could be more than 200 men working on one field.

This piece-work method of paying was not popular with everyone, particularly some of the village farm workers who had been used to being paid by the hour, a method which they felt gave them a chance to drag a job out without having to work too hard. One day, after telling them what the rate was for hoeing a row of carrots, Murfitt was standing in his office when he heard an argument going on outside. He saw Syd Williams, whom he had just taken on as a labourer, pinning one of the other men against the wall and telling him in forthright fashion, 'Look, I reckon the boss has offered us a fair deal on that hoeing. If we put our backs into it we could earn a fair bit this week, so if you don't like it why don't you bugger off and let somebody else have the job. Just don't sod it up for the rest of us.' Not long afterwards Murfitt offered Syd the foreman's job and there were few arguments after that.

Neither was piece-work popular with the other farmers, who found they were losing men to Murfitt, especially those who didn't live in tied cottages. According to one story, the subject cropped up one day at Bury market when Murfitt was approached by a farmer who went through the niceties of welcoming him to Suffolk and suggested that Murfitt and his wife might like to meet some of the neighbouring farmers and their wives at a dinner party.

As they were about to part the other farmer said some of the farmers were worried about the way Murfitt was paying his workers. They had heard Murfitts' labourers were getting up to twice the minimum wage, which the farmers thought was too high already. Murfitt replied it was just a matter of business. The harder his men worked the quicker he could get the crops to market for a good price and if the men did well at the same time that was all right with him. The promised dinner invitation never arrived.

Ted Kydd, Bill Murfitt's chauffeur, with the Buick saloon

One of the big differences Murfitt found in living in Suffolk was that there appeared to be greater importance placed upon your family background and position in society than there was in the Fens. Suffolk had a social structure built up of many centuries of settled, mostly affluent existence, whereas the Fens, which had been created out of the marshes and bogs bordering on to The Wash by the drainage engineer Vermuyden from the 17th Century onwards, had not had time to build up a 'squirearchy'. There was no 'county set' in the Fens and very few ladies of the manor.

The difference in the two cultures could best be seen in Risby between the Murfitts and the Burrells. Bill Murfitt was direct, said what he thought, was loud in his tastes and had been educated more by the experience of life than in the classroom or the officers' mess. He didn't suffer fools gladly, from any social class. Reginald Burrell, who lived in elegant style in Risby Place, was certainly no fool and he had made a commercial success in introducing large-scale fruit farming in an area previously known mostly for its corn and sugar beet. His new large cold store, where fruit could be chilled and stored as soon as it was picked, to be sold later for higher prices, was a model of modern farming. However, he had family money behind him, a university education, two immaculate grass tennis courts which befitted an amateur county player, and his own squash court. At weekends, when Murfitt was on his houseboat, Burrell and his wife were content to sit in deckchairs at the end of their lawn watching the village cricket team play in his adjoining meadow, separated by a ha-ha from too close a contact. Any business with Murfitt would be done through Burrell's agent, Frank Gamble, who took all the day-to-day decisions on how the farm was run.

It was in their choice of cars, however, that the final difference was seen. Murfitt liked big modern cars which looked as powerful as they were and with as many fittings as the manufacturers would supply. That was how he had come to choose his black American Buick, which looked a gangster's cars from one of the rapidly increasing Hollywood films. Burrell's saloon, a square-bodied Austin, was not quite as large, nowhere near as new, and the interior, although spacious, was uncluttered. As his chauffeur drove it sedately along the roads of West Suffolk it did not shout that the owner had money, although everyone knew that he did.

Murfitt had joined the local hunt but lately had to give up riding because of his weight. His favourite sport was shooting and he had made friends with a group of jockeys and trainers from Newmarket with whom he was buying a shooting syndicate. It fitted in well with his other hobby, horse-racing, which took him to Newmarket and Ascot meetings as often as he could go. Gertrude did not enjoy racing and she did not mind if Bill took other women friends, although she had been surprised when, last autumn, Mary Chandler asked him openly one day if she could go with him to meetings and, a little reluctantly, he had agreed. The trouble that had arisen over the fur coat afterwards was no more than he deserved, Gertrude thought.

Four   **A visitor, with cake**

Four
A visitor, with cake

RISBY SAT SNUGLY ON GENTLY rising ground to the north as you drove between Bury St Edmunds and Newmarket. That was how the village got its name – the village on the rise. It had been there more than a thousand years and over that time it had gone about its business quietly and mostly happily, its life centred around the flint-walled church with its Norman round tower, its two village greens and its two pubs. In medieval times the road through the village had taken pilgrims on their way to the Abbey in Bury St Edmunds and the shrine of the martyred King Edmund. Now, it didn't have too many visitors as the gradually increasing traffic on the turnpike which skirted round the village took present-day travellers to Ipswich and the seaside towns to the east, and to Cambridge and London to the west, as quickly as their Ford Eights, Baby Austins, Morris Eights and motor coaches could carry them. It was a situation of which the villagers generally approved. The 200 people who lived in Risby were not inhospitable, but given a choice they preferred to get on with life among themselves.

The sudden death of Bill Murfitt on Tuesday had caused rumour and gossip to whip through the village, bandied around by customers in the two shops, the post office and the butchers. At night in the Crown and Castle and the White Horse pubs there had been hardly any other topic of conversation – why had the police appeared so quickly, why were they asking the domestic staff so many questions? Some said

Murfitt had suffered a heart attack, and no wonder they said, look at his weight. Others whispered they had heard he committed suicide, which didn't surprise one or two who had picked up the fact that there had recently been trouble between him and his wife. A select few who had connections with members of the Murfitt domestic staff hinted it might be worse than that but said they were not supposed to say anything.

As Murfitt's foreman, Syd Williams came in for a lot questioning, particularly about whether he thought the Murfitt family would carry on farming in Risby. He said he didn't know, but he wished he did because what happened to the farm could seriously affect the future for him, his wife Rose and their seven children. Life had been a little better for Syd and Rose since Murfitt had taken him on, first as a labourer and later, for a welcome increase in wages, in charge of the men. The couple had been through some hard times after Syd was invalided out of the Army following a gas attack at Ypres in 1915, and when he returned to civvy street he had decided that if the world was going to be a better place for people like him he had to join with others to achieve it. He had never hidden his socialist opinions or trade union membership at a time when both made it difficult to get work in the close-knit Suffolk farming community, still almost feudal in many ways. The only job he had been able to get before Murfitt moved to the village was at Clacton on the railways, which meant a 50-mile cycle ride home on a Saturday and a similar ride back on a Sunday night, often in terrible weather, leaving his wife and family to fend for themselves during the week. He knew one of the other farmers in Risby had warned Murfitt he had taken on a trouble-maker, but over the last few years boss and foreman had developed a mutual respect. The previous night Syd had sat up with Rose, worriedly discussing whether he would be out of a job again.

One of Syd's sidelines was the village's newspaper round, which he had started when he was out of work and which had grown to a reasonable little business as his wife and the older children delivered the papers round the village after collecting them from the first train into Risby at 7am. On the morning after Murfitt's death he scanned quickly through the East Anglian Daily Times and it was not until he got to Page 11 that he found a short report with a headline saying, 'Well-known Risby Farmer. Sudden Death of Mr William Murfitt'. The report below gave brief details of the farmer's death, told how Dr Ware had been summoned to the farm, and was followed by brief details of Murfitt's life. There was no mention of poison or of it being a suspicious death.

Murfitt's eldest son Leslie and his wife Ricky, who worked as a fashion buyer for one of the major West End stores, had driven from London to Risby the evening before. As Leslie had his own business in London to run it was arranged that at Quays Farm Syd Williams would organise the men's work and would help Mollie Targett in organising lorries to go to Covent Garden and the canning factories. Another employee worried about his future was a young Scot, Ted Kydd, Murfitt's chauffeur and mechanic who drove the farmer around in his Buick. Ted had served an engineering apprenticeship in Aberdeen but, unable to get a job, he had taken up taxi driving and one of his fares had been Bill Murfitt when the farmer was in Scotland on a business trip. They got talking in the cab and Murfitt had told him if he could get to Suffolk there would be a job waiting for him. When he first arrived he lived in one of the disused railway carriages Murfitt had bought and sited just outside the village for casual workers to live in. Now he had moved into digs in the village and was engaged to marry Edna Mason, a member of one of the village's longest-established families.

Ted had felt settled, until now. He doubted whether a new farmer coming in would want a Buick, let alone a chauffeur, and although Murfitt had been buying more and more machinery which needed maintenance and repair, a new owner might not think on the same lines. He also loved the job he had been doing, driving Murfitt to his many business and social engagements, especially the social trips where he had quickly learned to use his discretion and certainly not to talk about them later.

One story Ted told only to members of his family was about a somewhat hilarious arrangement he had with Murfitt when he was being driven in his Buick while sitting in the back seat with his wife or one of his lady friends, particularly after a good meal. Murfitt would lean forward and call out 'Cough, Kydd,' which the chauffeur did as loudly as he could while his boss relieved his internal pressures by passing wind in the hope his female companions would not hear.

Ted was one of those who had been questioned by the police on the morning of Murfitt's death and he had been asked where he had been the night before. He said he and Edna had been to the pictures in Bury St Edmunds and had cycled home just after ten o'clock. He was asked if they had seen anyone as they passed Quays Farm and he said they had not. At that time he could not understand the purpose of the question.

• •

On the morning after Murfitt's death the front doorbell rang at Quays Farm. Doris Howard the maid went to answer it and came back to tell Ricky Murfitt that Mrs Chandler from Hall Farm was at the door. Ricky went to meet the visitor and came face-to-face with a tall, smartly dressed woman wearing a wide fashionable hat and carrying a cake on a dinner plate. In a soft Scottish accent Mrs Chandler asked if she could see Mrs Murfitt and Ricky replied that her mother-in-law was lying down. Mrs Chandler then explained that Mrs Murfitt had given her some ingredients to make a cake for her some time ago and while she was doing some baking on Friday she made one for her. She was going to bring it round earlier but thought Mrs Murfitt might like it now 'to cheer her up a little'.

Ricky thanked her and took the cake. When she showed it to Doris Howard the maid expressed surprise at what she called Mrs Chandler's 'nerve'. She explained that Mrs Chandler and her employer, James Walker, often used to visit the Murfitts in the past to play cards, but after Mrs Chandler always kept winning Bill Murfitt became certain she was cheating and she and Walker had been banned from Quays Farm for some weeks now. Ricky Murfitt thought the matter strange, if trivial, and wondered if it was something she should mention to the police.

Five **Scotland Yard is called in**

Five
Scotland Yard is called in

On Thursday morning the West Suffolk Chief Constable Colin Robertson travelled to Scotland Yard, where he discussed the Murfitt case with the head of the Criminal Investigation Department, Superintendent Bell, and with Detective Chief Inspector Leonard Burt, who had been assigned to the Bury St Edmunds investigation. Burt had risen rapidly through the ranks of the Metropolitan Police to his present position and, bearing in mind the rural location of the case, Bell might have also considered it an advantage that Burt had an agricultural background – he often joked about his father being the best pig man in Hampshire.

Robertson also met the detective who was to be Burt's assistant on the case, Sergeant Reg Spooner. On first impressions he would have thought them an unlikely pair. Burt was trim, athletic, firm but quietly spoken with little trace left of his country upbringing. Spooner was an obvious Cockney, stout, tie flapping outside his creased suit, which was covered in white ash from the cigarette permanently in his mouth or between his fingers.

Burt and Spooner had first met on a case in 1933 just after Spooner had been made up to sergeant and he was always grateful for the help Burt had given him. Burt, in turn, knew that in Spooner he had a man with a fantastic memory for names, faces and places, who took detailed notes of every fact he came across and never threw them away.

The West Suffolk Chief Constable did not know it at the time, but for his investigation in Risby he was being given the Murder Squad's brightest prospects who would eventually become two of the organisations best-known names.

After lunch Burt and Spooner travelled to St Mary's Hospital, Paddington, to see Dr Roche Lynch, the Senior Home Office Analyst, who was studying Murfitt's poisoned organs and other evidence sent from Quays Farm.

He told them Murfitt had been healthy but fat, overweight, a non-smoker, a former heavy drinker who had become a moderate one. He had been poisoned by cyanide potassium or cyanide sodium, which were very similar, traces of which were contained in the Fynnon Salts still left in the tin. Murfitt had taken about ten grains of cyanide, about twice what would normally be needed to kill anyone. The effect of the poison would cause a victim to simply sink to the ground unconscious and to die, usually in about 15 minutes. The fact that Murfitt lasted more than 40 minutes was probably due to his size. Burt had worked with Roche Lynch before and knew he was a stickler for detail.

● ●

Murfitt's funeral had been arranged for Friday afternoon and the farm workers, after dealing with any essential jobs, were given the morning off after getting this advice from Syd Williams: 'Sunday suits, don't stay too long in the pub at lunchtime and let's have a good turn-out.'

In the farmhouse Gertrude Murfitt was looking through the cards and letters of condolence which had been arriving by every post as well as being delivered by hand at the door. One she picked up was from her nephew Tom who wrote, 'I fear you are going to miss him terribly, for in spite of all the funny things you have said, we all know you have absolutely worshipped him.' Gertrude tried to remember exactly what funny things she had said.

There were quite a few letters from firms and business contacts, such as one from Ransome, Sims and Jefferies, agriculture engineers, from whom Murfitt had bought much of his equipment. They paid tribute to his 'wide knowledge of mechanical farming' while, Gertrude noted with a little amusement, promising on the letterhead that they would send an illustrated catalogue post free. Similarly a fashion shop she dealt with expressed sympathy under a no-nonsense banner which declared, 'Terms Net Cash.'

One lady who had read in the newspapers of the circumstances of Bill's death, apologised for her intrusion and asked if there was any reason to think he had suffered from a weak heart like herself. 'I find that a dose of salts causes me to completely collapse and after reading of your husband's death I have vowed never to take them again,' she wrote.

From Dunbartonshire she received the information that Bill had told all the members of a shoot he had attended that he would die by a certain time, which had already passed, the writer adding that they had been discussing life insurance at the time. The secretary of the Subscription Rooms Club, Newmarket, wrote that Bill had been there the Saturday before his death and was his usual cheery self – a visit he had never mentioned to her, Gertrude reflected ruefully. The secretary of his Masonic lodge in Newmarket said he had been directed by the Worshipful Master and Brethren to convey deepest sympathy to her over the loss of a popular member adding, perhaps needlessly she thought, 'Unfortunately we did not see him as much as we would have liked'. A cold storage company from Colchester also expressed sympathy while simultaneously informing that they held in store for her nineteen brace of pheasants.

Geraldine Burrell, of Risby Place, said they had been shocked to hear of her terrible loss, coupling her comments with those of her husband who, she said, was away. Gertrude hadn't expected them to be at the funeral anyway, knowing it was a little below their class. The last letter she picked up intrigued her. It had been sent to the Risby rector, the Reverend Webling, enclosing a donation he had received to his Sick and Poor Fund in lieu of sending a floral tribute. It was signed by James Walker, also on behalf of Mrs Chandler, asking the rector if he would be good enough to inform Mrs Murfitt. Gertrude, who had been told of Mrs Chandler's visit with the cake, was glad the housekeeper had not called personally with the donation.

• •

Just before two o'clock the hearse stopped in the road outside Quays Farm and, while the family were assembling in order at the front gate, the undertaker's men moved the coffin out of the car's rear door and lifted it on to the shoulders of the six Murfitt employees who had been chosen to carry it to St Giles Church a hundred yards away. As they started off Syd Pettitt, the farm mechanic, said quietly over his shoulder, 'He's not as heavy as I though he would be, Syd'. 'You're right there,'

Williams replied. 'They reckon the other half of him is in London being tested for poison.'

The funeral procession went slowly up the road, past the village school where the governess, Annie Elford, had assembled her pupils in the front of the grey flint Victorian building as a mark of respect. She had always got on well with Murfitt, who allowed her to use his meadow at the back of the school to teach football and cricket to the boys and stoolball and rounders to the girls.

As a bell tolled at intervals for the 56 years of Bill Murfitt's life, the cortege passed through the wooden lych-gate into the churchyard, the path lined each side by some 80 of Murfitt's employees. The rector met the coffin at the church entrance and preceded it down the aisle as the organist, Miss Freeman, played a melancholy air while at the same time looking into the mirror she always kept fixed to the organ to keep an eye on the choir behind her. Detective Sergeant Willis, in plain clothes, stood at the back of the church, mentally noting both the faces he recognised and those he did not, while PC Carrington, in uniform, patrolled the path beside the church which led to the newly-dug grave.

Just behind the immediate family mourners were the cousins and nephews, including young Roger Morton, who only a day or so before Murfitt's death had driven down to talk with his second cousin about joining him in Risby helping to run the farm, a possibility that had now disappeared.

Gertrude joined in the singing for the first hymn, Rock of Ages, knelt for the prayers and listened attentively while the rector spoke of Bill's life, of his achievements in farming and how it had brought prosperity to the village. But the occasion was now too much for her and as the congregation stood to sing

Abide With Me she collapsed onto the pew behind her. One of her sisters and her husband came forward, lifted her from the seat and as the singing continued supported her on each side as they walked down the aisle, out of the door and down the path on to the road leading back to Quays Farm. By the time the mourners were filing out of the church behind the coffin on their way to the grave she was in her lounge, prostrate on the settee, sobbing and inconsolable.

In the churchyard the pall-bearers lowered the coffin into a grave lined with laurel leaves, forget-me-nots and other flowers from Murfitt's garden. After the family had paid their last respects they looked along the mound of wreaths surrounding both sides of the grave. Gertrude's was there – 'To my own darling husband from his heartbroken wife' and one with a poignant message, 'To my darling grandpop from his only little grandchild Ann (I loved him so)'. Among the others was one from Newmarket inscribed, 'With deepest regret from Harry Wragg, H A Jellis, Bobby Jones, Dick Perryman, TT Taylor and Phil Lancaster' – Murfitt's racing friends with whom he had been going to share a shooting syndicate.

• •

Chief Inspector Burt and Detective Sergeant Spooner had left London in the morning and arrived in Bury St Edmunds as the funeral was taking place in Risby. They had a meeting with the Chief Constable and his deputy and just before they left to book into the Suffolk Hotel news came from the village that Mrs Murfitt had collapsed in the church. Burt and Spooner, thinking this might be a good time to interview her, set off in the car the West Suffolk police had made available to them.

Six **Husband learns of
wife's affair**

Six

Husband learns of wife's affair

When I had time to read Burt's report in detail it was obvious that from the start Mrs Murfitt was the prime suspect. 'Murfitt was undoubtedly a man of loose morals, and throughout his married life had been intimate with other women, including servants,' Burt wrote, pointing to a possible motive of revenge by the farmer's wife. Gertrude Murfitt's family were annoyed when the two detectives arrived at Quays Farm to interview her not long after she had been led sobbing from the funeral. But for Burt it was an ideal opportunity to question her when her emotions were still raw, a situation that might lead to an early confession. After the first interviews Mrs Murfitt told her family she thought Burt was a gentleman but that Spooner was a 'bastard', an unusually strong word for her. The Scotland Yard men were using the 'soft man, hard man' approach to good effect.

BURT AND SPOONER QUESTIONED MRS MURFITT from late afternoon until 9.30pm on Friday, the day of the funeral, and returned the next day when they continued the interview until 4.30pm. At first Burt asked her, in his conversational style of interviewing, about the two days before Bill Murfitt died and she told him about the happy Sunday they had with Charlie and Elaine Browne and their young son on the houseboat Omega at Horning, on the Norfolk Broads. They had a picnic on deck, played cards and waved to people on passing boats before driving home in the Buick in the afternoon.

On the Monday she told Bill at breakfast that she was going to visit her sister in Wisbech. She left at about 10.45am and the drive took her just over an hour and a half. She arrived home about 7pm and soon afterwards Bill, who had spent most of the day at his other farm, at Ickburgh in Norfolk, drove up. Bill went out to do some pigeon shooting and they had supper together before she went to bed at about 9.30pm. Bill followed soon afterwards. On the Tuesday morning Bill got up around 5.30 and she stayed in bed until it was time to get up for breakfast, which she and Mollie Targett had started just before Bill came into the dining room. There had been nothing unusual about the morning until then.

At this stage Burt withdrew from the interviewing and Spooner took over. First the salts – how long had her husband been taking them? For a year or two, they had both taken them, Gertrude replied. The same ones? They used to take Kruschen Salts, but changed to Fynnon for the last month or so because they seemed to do them more good. Normally they had a glass each at breakfast. Why had she not taken any on the Tuesday morning? Gertrude replied, 'I didn't fancy them. To tell you the truth, I had some the day before and while I was out visiting my sister

Scotland Yard Detectives
Chief Inspector Leonard
Burt, on the right and
Sergeant Reg Spooner
arrive for the inquest at
Risby Village Hall

I felt uncomfortable in the stomach. I don't think it was the salts but I thought I would go carefully, just in case. Bill had them as usual on the Monday and he didn't feel any effects.' When was the last time before the Tuesday that she had not taken any salts? She said she could not remember, it might have been a couple of weeks or longer.

Then Spooner asked her about the last seconds before Murfitt had taken the salts. He wondered why, after she had remarked to Mollie Targett that something seemed wrong with the salts, she served them to her husband without mentioning it to him? Gertrude said she had tipped away the top of the salts which were discoloured and damp and she thought the rest would be all right.

Then a key question; why had she had the dining room tidied up so quickly, and the dishes washed, before the police arrived? – 'I didn't know he was dying. I didn't know there was anything in the salts. I thought he must have had a heart attack or something. I had the room tidied up because the doctor was on his way. It's the sort of thing you do.' Spooner could relate to the last point. He could recall from his early days in the East End of London how any woman, from however humble a home, would scurry round with a pan and brush and duster to make sure, as a matter of pride, that it was spick and span before the doctor arrived.

Burt's turn for questioning again, quietly asking he if she could help in building up a picture of her husband's life, as this could help their inquiries. How long had they been in Risby, had they been happy there, who were their friends, did she know if her husband had any enemies?

Gertrude, now more relaxed, said they had been at Quays Farm for around five-and-a-half years, she supposed they had been mostly happy. Bill had worked hard to provide well for the family and deserved to enjoy himself by going racing and shooting. Lately he had taken to breeding spaniels as gun dogs, which had been taking up an increasing amount of his time.

Burt picked up on her comment that during their time in Risby they had been 'mostly happy' – what about the times when there weren't? Gradually it came out. There had been gossip, Gertrude said. It was none of other people's business. 'There was this girl called Kay, she literally threw herself at him...' then she clammed up. Burt dropped the subject for then, but came back to it later. He could tell there was a lot more to come out.

Kay it appeared, was a gamekeeper's daughter and Bill came to know her when they lived in Chatteris. He had told Gertrude once that he had to go away on business but she found out later he had been away with Kay in a caravan. Gertrude had found letters in his pocket from the girl and she was so disgusted that she packed her case and was going to leave him, but he begged her not to. He said he had not been keeping the girl but had just been giving her presents. 'He really expected me to believe it. I was so angry that he took me for a fool,' Gertrude said.

Was Murfitt still seeing Kay before he died? No, Gertrude said. She had made him write to the girl to say he didn't want anything more to do with her but she wouldn't let him go. She wrote to him at his Newmarket club threatening to send his letters on to Gertrude. She also wrote to Gertrude saying that if she was not attractive enough for Bill she must expect to lose him. As far as Gertrude knew he had not seen her for a couple of years and she had heard Kay had gone off and married a wealthy husband in Essex. Gertrude said she despised Kay but in a way felt sorry for Bill, he just couldn't help the way he was. She recounted to Burt what one of her friends had said – that Bill had one large problem and he couldn't keep it in his trousers.

By the late Saturday afternoon, after two days of questioning, Mrs Murfitt looked exhausted, but Burt knew that it if he treated her carefully there was a lot more she would tell him. He agreed to let her rest the next day and to see her again on the Monday.

• •

The next morning Syd Williams collected the bundles of Sunday papers for his delivery rounds at Saxham and Risby railway station and checked through them for any reports on Bill Murfitt's death. He found only one, on the front page of the News of the World under the heading 'Wealthy Farmer's Death Mystery' covering a story of how the Yard detectives had been at Quays Farm the day before but with little new information. He cycled to Quays Farm and handed a copy to Leslie Murfitt, who read it while his wife was attending morning prayer at the village church and he showed it to her when she returned. The family knew then that they would soon be the centre of many more newspaper stories and they didn't welcome the fact.

Gertrude had told Leslie and Ricky much of what she had told the detectives in her interviews, including Bill's affair with the gamekeeper's daughter which they had known about. In fact Leslie and Ricky knew other stories about Bill Murfitt's womanising and had discussed their own suspicions whether

Gertrude might have poisoned him because she was jealous and wanted revenge. When she told them Burt would be returning to take a full statement they asked if she was going to tell them about another of his affairs. She knew what they meant – that business between Bill and her best friend, Elaine Browne. At first Gertrude was reluctant to agree to tell Burt about Bill and Elaine. It was in the past, she had promised her friend she would forget all about it, she said, and she was not going to let her down. But Leslie and Ricky persuaded her it would be best if she told the detective everything, otherwise if they heard it from someone else they might think Gertrude had something to hide. The three of them also agreed that Elaine should be told of Gertrude's intentions when she and Charlie visited them, as planned, that evening.

• •

Ever since she had known her, Gertrude Murfitt had both admired and envied Elaine Browne. While Gertrude was short and slightly built with a pert, elfin-like face, Elaine was tall with a good figure and a well-structured face that could change from a haughty glance to a dazzling smile in seconds. Gertrude dressed smartly if sometimes over-fussily, Elaine went for simpler but superbly-cut costumes and dresses and dashing hats tilted at whichever angle the 30's fashion decreed. Gertrude's conversation centred round her home and family, with strangers she was hesitant and almost shy until she got to know them. Elaine could talk on any topic to anyone, was witty and she had the confidence of being a businesswoman in her own right as the owner of well-regarded fashion shops in Ipswich and Bury St Edmunds. She often went to London to fashion shows and to visit wholesalers and when she returned Gertrude was fascinated by the uproarious tales of the people she had met there. Bill had come home from Bury Market more than three years ago and said he had met Charlie Browne and had invited him and his wife over to supper. When they came a few days later Gertrude had been captivated by Elaine and, she had noticed with a little concern, so had Bill.

The Browne's arrived just after tea and it was while Charlie Browne was chatting to Leslie Murfitt that Gertrude told Elaine she was going to tell Burt about the affair. Elaine was horrified, but Gertrude said Sergeant Spooner already seemed to think she had given her husband poison so she had nothing to lose. She thought it best that Elaine admitted the affair to the detectives.

Elaine knew then that news of the affair between her and Bill Murfitt had to be broken to her husband, who until then had known nothing about it. She couldn't bring herself to tell him directly so she asked Ricky if she would do so. Ricky went into the lounge, took Charlie's elbow and led him into the garden. It was a perfect spring evening. The sun was casting its last light at the end of the garden and the midges were dancing into the fading rays with a promise of tomorrow. The bells of St Giles church were in their last phase of summoning the congregation for evensong and the murmur of conversation came over the wall into the garden as some of the less godly villagers made their way towards the Crown and Castle pub in time for the seven o'clock opening.

Ricky and Charlie stood under the large fir tree which dominated the garden. As they talked Charlie at first became agitated,
then angry, then he slumped down on to a garden bench, his
head in his hands and his shoulders shaking. Then he got up,
took Ricky by the arm and led her into the house. There were
still tears in his eyes as he walked over to Elaine and took her
by the hand.

Seven **Mrs Murfitt's secret diary**

Seven

Mrs Murfitt's secret diary

Although Bill Murfitt's affairs with the gamekeeper's daughter Kay and Elaine Browne were mentioned during the inquest on him later in the summer, and reported at the time, the full emotional drama contained in Gertrude Murfitt's revelations to Chief Inspector Burt about her husband's philandering were known only to close members of the family. The details, kept secret for more than 60 years, are described both in Burt's report and in copies of statements made to him by Mrs Murfitt during his investigations.

Also, during the time of her deepest unhappiness, Gertrude kept a diary in which she wrote of the anger and hurt her husband had caused her and the extract published in this chapter is attached to Burt's report. Even her closest family were unaware of its existence.

• •

WHEN SHE MARRIED BILL, GERTRUDE took on the typical role of the successful farmer's wife, staying at home and organising the domestic staff, bringing up the children, making sure the gardener produced enough fruit and vegetables and at the right time. She had not kept chickens, one of the ways many farm wives provided themselves with pocket money, or ran a dairy because there had always been enough money to buy what food she wanted. Sometimes she felt life was a little dull and she had wistful memories of her girlhood years when she lived at the pub in Wisbech, where her father was the landlord. He was a jovial, erratic character, fond of gambling. When his horses lost the pub was quiet, but if he won he came home with the money spilling out of his pocket and he wanted everyone, including the customers, to celebrate with him. As a farmer's wife Gertrude had felt she had a social position to maintain and she had been content to live in the shadow of her ebullient husband. Now, however, although his death had left her numb and shocked, in the last couple of days she felt a surge of power in her life. Her family were looking to her for a lead, she was the one the police needed to talk to, even if it was because they suspected she was a poisoner.

When Burt arrived on the Monday morning he began by asking her about the Fynnon Salts – who would know that she and Bill took salts every morning and who would know that the tin was normally kept on the sideboard? All the staff in the house would know, she told him, so would close friends like Elaine and Charlie Browne, and also Jim Walker and Mrs Chandler who had been frequent visitors up to March that year. The two Murfitt boys, obviously, but both were away at the time. He asked her where she had bought Fynnon Salts, and when. She was unable to remember exactly, probably she had bought a tin a couple of weeks ago from Leesons the Chemists in Bury St Edmunds and Bill had brought a tin home before then. Burt casually turned the conversation to cyanide – how could it have got into the salts, who would have access to it in the first place, and why?

Gertrude was adamant that she had never bought any cyanide, or any other poison for that matter. She knew that if you bought any you had to sign the Poisons Register and she had never needed to. Also, she was not aware that Bill had ever bought any, well perhaps some rat poison about two years ago. It was possible that some of the men on the farm had used some to destroy wasp's nests last summer. If Bill had bought any he would have probably have locked it away, possibly in his wine cupboard. She was willing to show Burt where it was.

Burt knew that while they spoke Spooner and other policemen were inspecting Poisons Registers in chemists shops in Bury St Edmunds and that his sergeant was probably in Mr Leeson's shop in Abbeygate Street at that moment asking if the chemist or his staff remembered anyone from Risby buying cyanide for any purpose over the last few months.

Burt then turned to the Murfitt's personal life, where he had left off on the Saturday evening. The girl called Kay, for instance, had she ever been to the house. Gertrude was indignant, even Bill wouldn't have had the cheek to do that to her, she said. What about other women, he asked. Have there been any others recently, do any of them live locally? Gertrude hesitated and then, as they sat in the garden, it all came out in a torrent of words.

'It started about three years ago,' Gertrude began. 'One evening when I received a telephone call, it was a woman saying that if I went to the Shire Hall in Bury St Edmunds I would see my husband with a lady friend. I didn't recognise the voice. Bill had said from time to time that he had met Elaine Browne at various events he went to but I knew Elaine had a busy social life and until then I was never suspicious. She had even been on holiday with Bill and me several times. When Bill came home that night I told him about the telephone call, but he denied there was anything in it. I tackled Elaine about it later, but she too denied she had been going out with Bill. After that I received more anonymous calls saying that Bill was out with "the Fornham lady" and there were rumours, which always came back to me... things like they had been spotted together in the back of the Buick, parked on the road somewhere between here and Fornham. After that, if she had been here alone visiting me and Bill offered to drive her home I made a point of going in the car with them. He didn't seem very pleased, if I remember.

Gertrude stopped talking but Burt persuaded her to continue. 'I had them followed and although they were never found in suspicious circumstances I knew they were serious about each other. About a year after my suspicions were first aroused I decided to have it out with both of them at the same time, and I received a terrible shock. Elaine admitted she and Bill had been lovers and that she had become pregnant. Bill had given a woman £5 for the address of a doctor to go to in London and afterwards Elaine had a miscarriage. I didn't know what to do, I was so bitterly unhappy. I told them I wanted a divorce, at least that would mean that he could go away with her and I could get out of their lives.

'They were both horrified. Elaine beseeched me not to do anything of the kind as she had two children and had no intention of breaking up my home. She even tried to say that she had been with Bill so that he would keep away from other women and not cause me any more unhappiness, as he had done with that girl Kay. Then Bill pleaded with me not to go. He said he would drink himself to death if I left him and both of them promised they would do no such thing again. I felt awful, but after a day or so I thought what's the point. I valued my friendship with Elaine and I had a comfortable life here, so I let the whole matter drop. It seemed the easiest way out.'

Burt asked if Murfitt and Mrs Browne had now ended their affair. 'I just don't know,' Gertrude said. 'I thought they had, then I began to wonder. After something like that has happened to you, you never stop being suspicious, it is like an evil that is always with you. I had them followed again from time-to-time, and I know they were still meeting.'

Burt asked if there was anything else Gertrude wanted to tell him. She got up, asked him to wait and walked off into the farmhouse. She returned with a book in her hand. It was her diary, she said, as she handed it to Burt.

Which part did she want him to read? She told him to try the December before last. With Christmas coming up she had been so depressed that she wanted to go away and forget it all, yet it would have been impossible. Burt opened the book and read the neat, sometimes unpunctuated writing.

December 24, 1936

'B. went to meet her after she left the hairdresser. Man saw him get into Elaine's car, by-road leading to Bonner's house, between Westley X-road and Saxham Church, 11.15am, and is willing to go to Ollard's to say what happened.'

'Ollard's?' questioned Burt – 'Oh, he's my solicitor.'

'Bonner?' – 'He's Lord Bristol's agent.' Burt read on.

'Bill quite exhausted on the journey to Bristol, same old thing all over again. I had relied on her keeping her word. Should never have done so. Could so easily have got free from him with all the other evidence and letters to produce. Have had nothing whatever to do with Bill since I knew about this. Why am I trying to shield her when she has ruined my life? Thinks if she marries Bill she might be able to keep him faithful, anyhow I have failed completely. Must tell somebody, just feel I cannot bear it, up to the present have not let anyone know, just thought for the sake of the children would bear it. Dare not let my little Billy know, I am sure he would do some terrible injury to Bill and to her and I have tried so hard to tell him all he has heard is not true.'

There was an entry covering the period January 10 to February 3, 1937. A thought ran through Burt's mind as to what kind of Christmas they all had.

'Went to Jack Ollard to get advice but would not say who the woman was, he wants me to take the man over to tell him what he saw. When I do this it will be the end of all things, Holman's letters are in his safe any time I need… they are willing to come and swear that all they have written down is perfectly true.'

Burt assumed Holman was a private investigator.

'I do wish they would decide to marry each other I feel it is slowly killing me, surely I am not meant to suffer like this. What will Charlie Browne do? I wonder if it will be as great a trouble to him as it has been to me.

I do wish I had gone when I first knew, perhaps by now I should be happy and glad to be freed, how can people be so cruel. I do try to remember that Elaine was kind to me when my other trouble was on but why didn't she finish this then.

He is a lustful brute. Why do such men marry, I hope that if anything happens to me my letters to him will make him faithful to his next partner. Anyhow he will, I think, realise that I have been a pal as well as a broken hearted wife.

Surely no man could be so vile to force a woman against her will, I try not to let myself think this of him. Things in his diary are vile it breaks my heart, especially those that I know are true.'

Burt stood quietly with the diary still in his hand. A loose sheet of paper fell to the floor. He picked it up and Gertrude said, 'That's a letter I left for him one night on the bed. I know he read it, but he left it on the bed in the morning and never mentioned it.' Burt read the letter.

'Bill, dear, You will never know how much you have hurt me, I do understand you do not want me as a wife. I have gone to sleep in Ann's room and then when I start to cry because I am so unhappy I shall not disturb you. I should hate to keep you awake because I know you have such a lot of worry, you must get your sleep otherwise you will not keep fit and strong and healthy and it has never been my wish to injure or hurt you in any one way.

I know lately that you have nearly fallen out of bed so that you should not be near me but you cannot say I have tried to worry you in anyway, but it just hurts and hurts and hurts and I have got such a lot deep down in my heart that you do not know and some days I can hardly bear it. Goodnight my dear, your loving Gertrude.'

Burt had never considered himself an over-sensitive man, but he would have felt both a sadness and compassion for Gertrude Murfitt. Many wives with a stronger will would have left a husband like Murfitt a long time ago but she had stayed with him, almost shackled in a medieval way. He said he would like to take the diary with him and she agreed.

In his rapid rise through the ranks of the Metropolitan Police Burt came to know there was no substitute for calm, meticulous police work in solving crimes, how fact built upon fact until they led to a logical conclusion. He knew the facts were all against Gertrude Murfitt, and after reading her diary he knew he would never have difficulty in proving that she had a strong motive to kill her husband. But he also knew from experience the importance of something less logical, of trying to find out how his suspects' minds worked, what their attitude was to being questioned and whether they showed fear or resentment at coming under suspicion. True, Mrs Murfitt had been hysterical and acted irrationally immediately after her husband's death but since then she seemed to have wrapped herself in a cocoon-like calmness, almost apathy, which he had not found in many others he had gone on to charge with serious crimes.

Eight **Where poison is a household commodity**

Eight
Where poison is a household commodity

LEONARD BURT HAD QUICKLY ADOPTED an early morning routine since moving into the Suffolk Hotel. He would have a quick bath, dress and walk out of the still-quiet hotel for a quick-paced walk around the medieval grid of streets that made up the centre of Bury St Edmunds.

He prided himself on keeping fit – the Metropolitan Police records showed that in his younger days he had been the force's sprint champion for a number of years – and whenever possible he liked to go for a brisk walk before starting the day. As he strode down the Buttermarket into Abbeygate Street and towards the ruins of the old abbey he thought how much alike England's market towns were. He came from one himself, in Hampshire, where he had taken his first job as a clerk with the local council, and he knew the effect a murder investigation, like the one now starting into Murfitt's death, would have on a closely-knit, perhaps inverted community like Bury St Edmunds.

At the age of 19 young Burt had tired of office life in the small town of Totton and went out looking for excitement and a job with prospects, both of which he found when be joined the Met. In his first posting, to Hoxton, one of the tougher parts of inner North London, he was sent to a pub – he remembered the name of it still, the King of Prussia – where two men had been relieving some of the customers of their hard-earned money and valuables while inflicting no little physical injury in the process. The men were pointed out to him and when he went to arrest one of them four other men jumped on him. He got one villain on the side of his head with a truncheon but the others kicked him to the ground and put the boot in until he was almost unconscious. Just as they were giving up Burt staggered up, set off in pursuit of one of the gang and cornered him in a garden. They were still wrestling in the moonlight when he was saved by the arrival of other policemen from the local station, who had been told of the fight by one of the crowd. He had received his first commendation for that and, because of his injuries, a move to Scotland Yard on clerical duties before being sent to a quieter posting in South London. He had never forgotten, though, how the majority of the crowd outside that Hoxton pub had watched him being methodically beaten up without coming to his aid, a salutary lesson for the boy from the country that the British bobby was not always as popular as some people would have you believe.

Not long afterwards he joined the CID as a detective constable in Bow and a combination of hard work and a shrewd, methodical mind helped him quickly through the ranks to sergeant and inspector before joining the Murder Squad in 1936 as a chief inspector.

One of his biggest successes had been the case which became known as the Charing Cross Trunk Murder, in which the body of a woman was found in the London rail terminal's left luggage office after staff noticed a peculiar smell exuding from a wickerwork trunk. Burt found the body had been cut up into five parts, each piece carefully wrapped in brown paper and tied with string. It was only painstaking work by Burt and another detective which led to the discovery of a bloodstained match-stick which in turn led them to arrest the killer. It was in that case that he first worked with Dr Roche Lynch, who had impressed him by the way he had cut up the suspect's suit into little pieces and tested each piece for bloodstains which matched those on the matchstick. Burt remembered, wryly, that he had to lend the man, John Robinson, one of his own suits which he wore in court and later as he walked to the gallows to be hanged.

Because of his rural background Burt liked to get out of London for his cases, unlike some of his fellow officers. One that had given him great satisfaction was when he was sent in January 1937 to Newark, in Nottinghamshire, where a ten-year-old girl, Mona Tinsley, had gone missing. Despite a huge search, a radio appeal and the 20-mile dragging of a main canal police had been unable to find her body. They had, however, built up enough evidence against Frederick Nodder, a one-time lodger with the girl's family who had been seen with Mona just before she disappeared, to have him jailed for seven years for abduction in the March. Inevitably, the usual posse of water diviners, clairvoyants and astrologers came forward with their theories. Most, as usual, were completely wrong, but an astrologer from Bristol predicted that Mona's body would be found in June in the River Idle, 30 miles north-west of Newark in open mead-owland with tall trees lining the bank. In the first week of June, after Burt had returned to London, Mona's body was found in just such a spot. She had been strangled. Burt returned to Nottinghamshire to question Nodder, who had previously refused to go into the witness box to give evidence. Nodder then decided he would have to speak to try and save his skin, but the story he gave to the court was muddled and unbe-lievable, and he had been hanged in Lincoln Jail before

Christmas. Burt, always sceptical about the unwanted help of soothsayers and the like, still believed the astrologer's prediction was a coincidence. In some cases the detective could strike a bond of near friendship with some of his suspects because of his quiet, reasoned questioning, but for Nodder he felt only disgust for his murder of a happy, innocent little girl.

It was not just the dark world of violent death that had made Burt's time in the Murder Squad fascinating. There had been the case of the forged will of a theatrical wig-maker, which had involved blackmail of an Indian Maharaja and which had ended only a few months ago in the perpetrators going down for long jail sentences. And there had been the hunting down of a rich young man who had sent extremely indecent letters addressed to 'The Head Girl' of one of our most select public schools, asking her to carry out a coded correspondence with him through personal advertisements in the Daily Telegraph. Burt had replied through the column, using his own name, and had set up a meeting with the man in Harrods, using a policewoman in plain clothes as a decoy. The dirty letter writer received six months, far too lenient, thought Burt, for a man who it transpired had been setting out to corrupt both boys and girls in schools throughout the country.

. . . .

While Burt had concentrated on questioning Mrs Murfitt on the Monday, Reg Spooner and the local police talked to every member of the domestic staff at Quays Farm about what had happened the night before Murfitt died. As a result the mundane life of very ordinary people was sifted over and analysed for any possible clue.

Doris Howard, the maid, and Beatrice Cutmore, the cook, had to think hard when asked by Sergeant Willis what time they went to bed. They eventually remembered it was about 10.15, just after they had finished listening to the New Variety Show on the wireless featuring The Two Leslies, The Trix Sisters, Scott and Whaley, and others.

Doris said that before going to her room she had locked the front door and one of the back doors, leaving a side door unlocked so that Mollie Targett, who was out at a party with her fiancé, could get in. Mrs Murfitt was in bed and as the light was on in the dining room she assumed Mr Murfitt was in there. Mollie Targett said her fiancé drove her home from the party at Lavenham and dropped her off in the farmyard at about 11 o'clock. She had not noticed anything unusual when she came in.

The chauffeur, Ted Kydd, remembered the night well as he and his fiancé Edna Mason had cycled home at about 10.30 after going to the Odeon cinema in Bury St Edmunds, where they had seen Jack Benny and Ida Lupino in Artists and Models. They saw nothing untoward as they cycled past the farm and thought all the lights were off.

Burt and Spooner took it upon themselves to check Kydd's story with his fiancé, who worked in the next village, Fornham All Saints, as cook to the Gough family. Edna Mason answered the bell and went to tell her employer that two policemen were at the front door and wanted to talk to her. Mrs Gough, who thought a policeman's place was at the back door, rushed out to tell the two detectives they could not come in, but by this time they were already in the hall and proceeding towards the kitchen. Edna's story coincided exactly with that of the chauffeur and she added for good measure, 'You can't possibly think my Ted has done anything. Mr Murfitt was a good boss and he thought the world of him.'

. . . .

In a boarding school in the seaside town of Birchington, in Kent, eight-year-old Ann Murfitt was called to the head-mistress's study, where a detective from the local force asked her if she had stayed with her grandparents at Quays Farm recently. The little girl replied that she had. The detective asked solemnly if she could tell him if her grandfather took health salts every morning and Ann replied, equally solemnly, that he did. She was then allowed to go back to her classroom.

In the Norfolk Village of Saham Toney, Albert Leeks was packed and ready to move. He had given in his notice to the farmer for whom he worked as pigman and, with his wife Maud, twin sons Sonny and Percy, aged 14 and his eight-year-old daughter Marjorie, was looking forward to a new life in Risby, some 30 miles away. In the post came a letter from Mollie Targett telling Albert that, because of the unfortunate death of Mr Murfitt, they could not now guarantee him the job to which he had been appointed. The Leeks family were to wait several weeks before they knew what their future would be. (They did in fact move to Risby where they lived happily for many years.)

. . . .

By a week after Murfitt's death, the routine life of the village was being interrupted continually by the police's investigations. They went into Murfitt's barns and cattle sheds, pulling hay out of the mangers, sorting through sacks of cattle feed, emptying dustbins, asking the bemused farm workers if they had seen any strange tins or bottles which might have contained poison. At one point Doris Howard was called out to the dustbins at the back of the house where Sergeant Bigmore had found a pile of Hoover sweepings. She had to identify it as that which she had collected from various rooms in the house on the day of Murfitt's death. Schoolchildren out during the morning play break watched in awe as a huge lorry trundled past clanking with the contents of the village rubbish dump, a favourite play area for the village lads. The lorry went off to Bury St Edmunds, where reluctant constables sorted out six tons of the tins, one by one, without coming across anything suspicious.

The pond outside Quays Farm was drained and others in the village searched with rakes and nets. A ditch running alongside the road towards Jim Walker's farm was searched by a dozen shirt-sleeved policemen. When the school turned out, several of the boys enthusiastically joined in until the policemen told them, in no uncertain manner, to go away. There was, however, one sign of rivalry in the police force. A sergeant said to one passing villager, 'Don't forget, if you see a bottle or a tin which looks as though it might have had poison in it then tell us first, and not these boys from London.'

The gardener, George Howard, was asked if he ever used cyanide. Yes, he said, last year they had several wasps nest on the farm and Mr Murfitt gave him a small bottle of the poison to do away with them. He had buried the bottle afterwards, but he could not remember where. Syd Williams said he had not bought any cyanide for about ten years but he had helped his brother Dick the previous year when he had used some to destroy a hornet's nest. The thorough Spooner walked the two brothers through the village to Dick's cottage in South Street, where the door was opened by his surprised wife, Miriam. Dick took Spooner through to the scullery where he took a small bottle of cyanide from the top of a food safe. After careful examination Spooner declared himself satisfied the bottle had not been recently opened, but he took it away for further examination all the same. Miriam made a pot of tea and it was another half hour, after the four of them had tasted some of her newly-baked scones and chatted about life in the village, before the cosy little party broke up. A couple of days later Dick and Miriam were surprised to see the detective's visit to their cottage recorded in detail on Page 3 of the Daily Mirror under the heading 'Poison for 100 on Farm' and telling how a bottle almost full of cyanide was now in the hand of Chief Inspector Burt.

Norfolk police were asked to go to Horning, on the Broads, to search Murfitt's houseboat which he had bought for £300 just before Easter. They reported back that they had found some bottles of drink, cans of vegetables, a pack of cards, but no cyanide.

• •

In Bury St Edmunds all five of the town's chemist shops were visited by the West Suffolk police. They found that since April the year before there had been a total of 425 purchases of cyanide, in various forms, while in neighbouring Newmarket there had been 145 sales of the poison in the same period.

'That's bloody astounding,' Burt said when Spooner gave him the details. 'They use it round here like a household commodity. Do you realise that for less than a shilling you can buy enough cyanide to kill a hundred people, just as long as the chemist knows you and you sign the Poisons Register. It's a wonder there's anyone left alive around here.' He said he would ask the local police to follow up every sale.

Burt then asked Spooner how he had got on at Leesons, the chemists which they knew the Murfitts used. Spooner said Bill Murfitt bought a one ounce bottle of cyanide on September 4th last year and a four ounce bottle on September 8th. How about Mrs Murfitt, Burt asked. Mrs Murfitt bought a one ounce bottle of cyanide there on September 7th, when she signed the Poisons Register, he said. The chemist said it would still be usable now.

The detectives returned to Quays Farm to ask Mrs Murfitt why she had told Burt she had never bought any cyanide, when the records revealed she had bought some on September 7th. She said if she had signed the Poisons Register then she must have bought the poison, although she had no recollection of it. If she had bought it would have been because her husband asked her to.

• •

Proof that Mrs Murfitt had indeed bought cyanide when she had told Burt that she had not done so increased the evidence that was accumulating against her, but Burt was still not yet convinced she was the murderer and certainly he did not have enough evidence to charge her. There was no proof she had put the poison in the salts, her explanation of why she ordered the dining room to be cleared could be seen as a decision a woman would naturally take in preparation for a doctor's visit and a jury would be quite likely to believe that a recently bereaved widow would not be able to remember a purchase of poison she had made some months ago. But if not Mrs Murfitt, who was the killer?

Nine Spooner's night at the village pub

Nine
Spooner's night at the village pub

ON THE TUESDAY AFTERNOON, a week after Murfitt's death, Burt
caught the train from Bury St Edmunds to London, where he
had to attend a legal conference the next morning on one of
his previous cases which was coming up for appeal. Spooner
had an early dinner at the Suffolk Hotel and went up to his
room.

Reginald Spooner had decided he wasn't particularly enjoying
this case. He didn't like the country – he didn't think it was a
natural place to live. He didn't feel secure here, as he did in
London where he was born and brought up and where he had
spent all his working life. You knew where you were in London,
the buildings, although grubby, gave you natural boundaries,
the streets didn't change colour with the sunrise and sunset.
Everyone had told him of the big open skies he would see in
Suffolk, of the flat but still beautiful countryside. But he preferred his skies limited by the silhouettes of rooftops while
the countryside, full of May pollen, only gave him hay-fever.

And there were the people. In London there was a camaraderie
about the place, even among the villains, that once you linked
into it could give you almost an unlimited amount of the information, hints and sidewinks that were essential to the work
of a detective. He had now been 14 years in the Force and
throughout he had made a point of making, if not always

friends, at least contacts among all the communities in which he worked. Sometimes he knew he had to trade with some very dubious characters to get the information he wanted, but it was all part of the job.

He had started his working life as an insurance clerk and only thought about being a policeman because he considered it a more secure job. When he appeared before the Metropolitan Police selection board he was lucky enough to be able to cite the example of his great grandfather, Charles Lockerby, who had been one of the original Peelers in the 1880s, and he was careful to include all his first names, Reginald William Lockerby, on his application form. At first the life of Constable Spooner on uniformed beat in the crowded, noisy streets of Hackney did not really appeal to him, but by building up a network of informers he received a growing list of commendations on his personal file and he was soon attached to the CID, where he had the joy of working in civvies. By the time he became a full detective ten years ago he was recognised, among both the crooks and his colleagues, for painstaking, detailed investigation, the copious notes which he assiduously filed away for immediate and future use and for his patient but not always polite interrogation. It made him, his superiors noted, the perfect witness in court, unfazed by defence counsels' quibbling and sometimes malicious cross-examination.

But here in Suffolk, where life and the people moved at a different pace, Spooner felt uneasy. He had no contacts and it was difficult to get to know the locals. He knew his London accent was against him and he tried to curb his use of Cockney rhyming slang which he could use in London to put him on the same conversational level of informers and suspects. In Suffolk, he discovered, they didn't even seem to talk much among themselves and what conversation they had was interrupted by long periods of ruminative silence. He had mentioned it only yesterday to one of the local sergeants who, unhelpfully Spooner thought, replied, 'Yes… (silence)… we don't talk much… (silence)… but we think a lot.'

Perhaps he had been feeling the strain of the long hours he had been putting in when he wrote home to his wife Myra that Bury St Edmunds was a lousy dump 'somewhere about 1200 years old and, by Jove, doesn't it look it.' This was his first investigation outside London since he rejoined the Murder Squad a few months earlier and he missed The Smoke more than he realised.

Spooner knew when he arrived that the type and scale of crime in Suffolk was completely different to that of London. In one of his first cases in the East End, he had helped to convict a couple of blackmailers who went inside for five years and he now considered that one of his more minor successes. In Suffolk that would have been one of the biggest crimes they had dealt with in years. In another investigation in Bow he went in search of the killer of a cinema manager who was found battered by an axe and Spooner's damning evidence played a large part in sending the murderer to the gallows. When, earlier in 1938, he had been made head of the Yard's anti-pornography squad he thought life might become quieter but he then found he was in contact with some of the most unsavoury characters in Soho for whom violence was an essential part of their business. There weren't too many people like that around Bury St Edmunds.

The pubs, too, were totally different. In London they played a big part in his life for meeting contacts and for celebrating successes with his fellow officers. Burt, with whom he had previously worked in London, had remarked that there were few pubs Spooner went into where he didn't know someone. He always stood at the bar, never sat, and always positioned himself near one of the ornate mirrors so that without making it obvious he could watch who was coming and going and, more importantly, who was drinking with whom. Suffolk pubs had smaller rooms, few mirrors and were full of nooks and crannies so that you couldn't see what was going on.

That evening Spooner, on a sudden whim, decided to drive out to Risby for what he called a 'nose around.' He parked the car on the side of the top green and walked around the village, nodding to one or two people he had already interviewed, but they gave no sign that they wanted to stop for a conversation. Wondering if he had done the right thing, he then decided to go into the Crown and Castle where at least he would have the company of a pint of Greene King's bitter, which he had begun to appreciate.

There was a spring chill in the air and the light was fading as he opened the pub door. Oil lamps gave off pungent fumes and wisps of acrid smoke were coming from a newly-lit coke fire. He walked along a narrow passage with stairs on one side and a room on the other which the landlady used as a grocer's shop. At the end of the passage was a small, rather cosy parlour with padded chairs against the walls and tables in the centre, and from that a curtained opening to a larger saloon with smoke-engrained walls and ceiling, sawdust on the floor and furnished with rough wooden tables and benches. Two young men were playing darts while four older men sat disconsolately round a table, sharing between them one pint of beer which they supped in turn. Spooner had heard of this custom in London, which had grown out of necessity during the various periods of poverty working men had suffered, but he did not think it still existed.

There was no bar for him to lean against but from behind a curtain there appeared a large and amiable barman who took a look at Spooner's suit and asked if he would like to drink in the parlour. No thanks, Spooner said, he'd have one here – and while he was about it would the other gentlemen in the bar care for a drink as well. There were looks of surprise, the curt nodding of heads and the barman disappeared again behind the curtains. While he was gone Spooner tried to strike up a conversation, bringing in the fact that he was looking into Murfitt's death and that he wanted to speak to anyone in the village who might help him. By the time the barman reappeared, this time with a separate pint for each man in the saloon, it seemed as if he had slightly breached an unseen barrier and a slow but reasonable conversation began with the four older men.

At this point one of the two young darts players walked across to them and said aggressively, 'Here, did you say you're one of them detectives working on the Murfitt case?' Spooner said he was. 'Well, I reckon you've got a bloody cheek asking for help here,' the young man spat out.

Spooner asked why and automatically offered him a cigarette, which the young man took and put behind his ear.

'Look at what your lot did to me,' said the young man and produced from his wallet a recent newspaper cutting from the local newspaper, the Bury Free Press. Spooner took it and read how one John Leonard, a labourer, had been found guilty of trespassing in search of game in a local wood, for which he had been fined ten shillings by the local magistrates, and also found guilty of assaulting and beating a gamekeeper, one Arthur Spalding, for which he was fined a further pound.

'Did you do it?' asked Spooner. 'After all, if you were out shooting game and beat up a gamekeeper I would say that's pretty serious in these parts.' 'Shooting!' the young man snorted. 'I was only using a bloody catapult, and old Moki Spalding came up on his bike afore I could hit one of his pheasants.'

'Then what about the beating up?' asked the detective.

'All I did, because I was so bloody angry, was to put my fist up in front of his face,' said the young man. 'I didn't even touch him. Do you call that a big crime? That fine was nearly a week's wages to me.'

Spooner thought of one of his previous cases when he had a seaman, about the same age as the young man in the bar, sent down for a razor attack on his prostitute girlfriend, who later died. By comparison young Leonard's misdemeanour seemed like a breath of fresh air.

'I see your point,' said Spooner. 'Fist up in front of his face, you say. In the pubs I use in London I'd reckon that would be normal Saturday night polite conversation.' He added, 'Anyway, if you do hear anything about Murfitt that might help I'd really like to know.'

The young man gave a surly grunt, took the cigarette from behind his ear and accepted Spooner's offer of a light.

Outside it was almost dark and the barman came in with another lamp. Spooner put his hand up, circled his finger and wordlessly indicated another round. The barman disappeared behind the curtain and a few minutes later came out again with a tray containing pints for all, including himself, and settled down on one of the benches.

The talk had turned to village gossip, in-jokes about the village football team which Spooner didn't understand but laughed at all the same, and to the next day's racing. There was a lull, then the conversation came round to Murfitt again.

'Can't think who could have done it,' one of the men said.

'How about Bill Thomson,' said another with a chuckle. 'He hasn't got a good word to say about Murfitt now.'

'Why's that?' asked Spooner, 'Who's Bill Thomson?'

'He's a shepherd,' said the first man. 'Murfitt sacked him and has been trying to get him out of his cottage ever since he went to look over his sheep one day and found Bill wasn't there. Bill's very bitter about it because he said he had just gone home for breakfast and would only have been away half an hour, but Murfitt wouldn't listen. Bill won't budge and I hear it may come to court.'

'Old Bill wouldn't murder no-one,' said another of the men. 'He don't even like his sheep being taken to market and you'll never find him eating mutton.'

'How about Jimmy Bennett, then,' said another. 'You know how he used to park his car at his son-in-law's in Heath Barn. Well not so long ago Murfitt heard that Jimmy had been putting round stories that he'd seen Murfitt knocking back the scotch at the White Horse and he had to get them to phone Ted Kydd to come and fetch him. Since then he's refused to let Jimmy park his car there and he's furious because there's nowhere else to park it in the village.

Spooner made mental notes. A shepherd about to lose his house and a man denied space to park his car – neither seemed strong enough motive for murder, but in the country you never knew.

Then young Leonard walked across again from the dartboard. 'How about Moki Spalding?' he asked. 'He's got a score to settle with Murfitt.'

'In what way?' asked Spooner.

'Well, for the last year he and Murfitt have been having a go at each other. Seems that Moki caught Murfitt shooting pheasants down at Heath Barn and reported it to the estate's office.'

'I thought Heath Barn was Murfitt's, said Spooner. 'Surely he's got a right to shoot what he wants on it.'

'That's where you're wrong,' said one of the older men. 'He only rents the land off of Hengrave Estates, who still have the shooting rights. Old Moki thinks the pheasants are his personal property and he gets right uppity if anybody starts knocking them off.'

'Yeah,' young Leonard said. 'Moki had a real go at Murfitt and the old boy didn't like it one bit. Then Murfitt got his own back by going to see Sir John Wood personally at Hengrave Hall to complain about Moki's attitude and asked for him to be sacked. Yeah,' he chortled. 'I reckon Moki did it.'

'What's this Moki like?' Spooner asked. 'Seems as though he's only doing his job.'

'Well sometimes he goes too far,' said one of the other men. 'Has anyone told you what he did to that car on Lackford Heath?

Spooner said no one had and he was soon enlightened. It appeared that Moki was out on patrol one night when he saw a car parked on the heath that separated Risby from the neighbouring village of Lackford. There was a young man in the driving seat and Moki, thinking he was there in search of a pheasant or a rabbit, asked him to get out. The young man just sat staring straight ahead as if in a daze, which infuriated Moki to the extent that he smashed the windscreen with his stick. A girl's head shot up from the level of the gear lever where it had previously been and let out a loud scream. The young man wound down the window and had a go at Moki, saying they were not doing any harm and what the hell did he think he was doing. He said he would report Moki to the police for malicious damage. Moki said that was all right with him – they shouldn't have been doing what they were doing anyway, and he would have no hesitation in telling anyone so. With that the young man drove away fast, with broken glass flying from his windscreen and the girl still screaming at the top of her voice.

By this time other village men had gradually filled the room for the last half hour of drinking time and there were laughs and sniggers all round. 'That's just like Moki,' said one. 'He don't like anyone enjoying themselves.'

'He sounds a bit of a character. I might have a word with him sometime', Spooner said. 'Does he come in here for a drink at any time?

This was met by even more laughter and one of the men said. 'Come in here! He knows that if he came in here for a drink there'd be nobody else left in the pub. We'd all be out there after his bloody pheasants.

Spooner joined in the laughter. As he got up to go young Leonard shouted out, 'Off to arrest old Moki then? I'll show you where he lives if you like.'

'Not tonight,' Spooner replied. 'I might get my car smashed up.'

He was still chuckling as he got into his car. It was the first night he had enjoyed since he left London. But before he drove off he pulled out his notebook and wrote himself a reminder that included the names Thomson, Bennett and Moki Spalding. You never know, he thought.

Ten **Mystery of the missing key**

Ten
Mystery of the missing key

THE MORNING AFTER HIS VISIT to the Crown and Castle Reg
Spooner drove out to Risby again. He had to drive slowly
through the centre of Bury St Edmunds, crowded with stalls
for the Wednesday street market, and into Risbygate Street
which was jammed with cattle trucks queuing up to offload
cows, sheep and horses at the weekly cattle market. Men pushed
handcarts loaded with wire cages full of live chickens and
women struggled along the pavements balancing boxes containing tame rabbits on prams and pushchairs. Farmers and
labourers sat patiently on horse-drawn wagons and tumbrils,
empty for now but which would be full on the return journey
of new stock and supplies for their farms. Some would hitch
up their horses on the edge of the market and go straight to
the pubs, which opened at ten o'clock for the rest of the day.
When they went home many would be merry or drunk,
probably fall asleep in the back of the cart and let the horse
find its own way home.

Spooner went to Quays Farm because he wanted to check
some of the statements the domestic staff had made immediately after Murfitt's death. Sitting in the farmhouse kitchen
he was stifled with heat from the Aga cooker and had to talk
loud enough to make himself heard above the whine of the
generator in the yard outside, which made it one of the few
houses in the village with electricity.

The detective asked the maid, Doris Howard, and the cook, Beatrice Cutmore, how they had gone about locking up the house the night before Murfitt died. Doris said she had locked the front door and the back door before she went to her room, Mollie Targett had locked the side door when she came in from a party she had been to with her fiancée. None of the staff had a key to the front door – it could be locked from the inside just by slipping up a catch on the Yale lock. There was supposed to be a catch which you could push up to stop it being unlocked by a key from the outside, but it didn't seem to work.

Did she check on the doors when she got up in the morning? Yes, said Doris, she always did. The front door was unlocked, but she thought Mr Murfitt might have opened it to look outside to see if the men were waiting at the gate to start work. The back door was unlocked, which was normal when Mr Murfitt was the first one up.

Who had keys to the front door? Mollie Targett told him Mr and Mrs Murfitt had one each and young Billy had been given one when he came home late one night, had been unable to get in and had gone to a friend's house to telephone his father to ask him to open the door. The local police had asked earlier about the keys and all three had been found, including Billy's which was in a drawer in his bedroom.

Then Mrs Murfitt, who had been listening to the conversation, told Spooner that another key had been made – when Bill decided to give one to Billy he actually ordered two. In January Bill had given her the second new key while he had a disc fitted to hers, and he returned her original one a couple of weeks later. He took the other key back and although they had hunted all through the house, including his things, they hadn't been

William Murfitt with his wife Gertrude on the right of the picture and his lover Elaine Browne

able to find it. Spooner thanked her and made some notes in his book, underlining the point about the missing key.

Spooner then asked the staff if they had heard anything unusual the night before Murfitt died. No, they all said in turn. How about in the weeks before then, had they noticed anything different at the farm? It was then that Spooner heard about a mystery woman seen walking in the road outside the farmhouse late at night.

Doris had seen her the Thursday before Murfitt died. 'It was about a quarter past ten. I'd been out to deliver a message for master and as I was coming back I heard footsteps and saw this woman walking past the house. She was dressed in dark clothes.' Spooner asked if Doris had recognised the woman. The maid wasn't sure, but she thought it was Mrs Chandler, from Hall Farm. 'It had made me very frightened and I ran home to tell Beatrice,' the maid said.

Then it was suggested that Spooner had a word with Ted Kydd, the chauffeur, who had also reported seeing a woman walking outside the farmhouse. The chauffeur said it had happened about three weeks previously. He was out cycling with Edna, his fiancée, at about 9.30 in the evening and as they passed the churchyard gate he saw this lady walking along the road towards the church. She must have passed the house just a few minutes before. 'I'm sure it was Mrs Chandler, I know her fairly well because I have often driven her in the car. She was wearing a fur coat and had no hat. I remarked to Edna that I wondered if she was all right because she was walking very slowly, but we didn't like to stop.'

Spooner made more notes in his book. He didn't know how this new information would help, but it would all have to be checked out.

• •

Since Mrs Murfitt's revelation to him about her husband's affair with Elaine Browne, Burt knew he would have to interview her and her husband, and he also knew it would not be a comfortable meeting. Their home, Moseley's Farm in Fornham All Saints, a village about three miles from Risby, was an imposing pink-washed farmhouse at a crossroads on the main road between Bury St Edmunds and Mildenhall, with the village pub just across the road and the church a couple of hundred yards away. It was the house of a man important in his village and probably outside as well, thought Burt, a man who would now be filled with horror at the thought of his family's personal life becoming public property, as he probably realised that it was likely to be.

Charlie Browne told them that on the Monday before Murfitt died he spent the whole day on his farm and didn't go within a mile and a half of Quays Farm. On the Tuesday he got up at 5.30am as usual but didn't go near the Murfitt's s home until he heard at about nine o'clock that his friend was ill, and later when he and his wife went to Quays Farm he learned Murfitt had died.

Burt then told him that Mrs Murfitt had told them about Elaine and Murfitt's affair and Browne said he had known nothing about it until Ricky Murfitt had told him in the garden on Sunday. Burt persisted, surely Browne must have had some idea, it seemed it had been the subject of gossip in Risby for some time. Browne said once or twice the thought ran through his mind, but he could never believe it. They were all such good friends.

Burt then said he had heard that at one time Browne had threatened to shoot Murfitt and the farmer denied it. 'I never quarrelled with Bill, Murfitt, never had any reason to do so. We were friends with them right up to the day he died,' he said.'

How had the Brownes first heard Murfitt was ill and how was it they came to be at Quays Farm so quickly? Browne told the detectives how his wife's maid made the telephone call to ask what time Elaine Browne was due to meet Mrs Murfitt for a shopping trip to Ipswich which they had planned while they were on the houseboat and when Mrs Browne took the phone she was told Murfitt had collapsed. They drove over to Risby immediately.

Burt then questioned him closely about his wife's movements the day before Murfitt died and he said she had gone to London with a friend at 8am and returned home between 7.30 and 8pm. On the Tuesday she did not get up until just before 9am.

How about cyanide, Burt asked, had he bought or used any recently? Browne said he had not bought any for at least 10 or 11 years and he had none in his possession now. Murfitt had given him a tin of poison gas two or three years ago to deal with some vermin on the farm, but although the detective asked him to show him the tin later he knew it was not the poison which had been found in the salts.

When Elaine Browne came into the room Burt noticed she was pale and nervous. He asked her when her association started with Murfitt and when were they first intimate. She said it started after Mrs Murfitt had asked her to use her influence over her husband to get him to break off the association with the girl named Kay. He stopped seeing the girl about two years ago, but it was then Elaine found Bill was fond of her. They had made love, but it stopped after they both admitted it to Gertrude.

'But were you still jealous over Mr Murfitt?' Burt asked. 'Mrs Murfitt says you told her that he was having an affair with his niece, Valerie Smythe, and you said that was why Murfitt had taken on her husband Jimmy as manager. You also made allegations about his conduct with Ricky Murfitt and Miss Targett, was any of that true?'

Elaine Browne broke down in tears. 'I might have said something of the sort to Gertie to get my own back on Bill, but never really seriously thought there was anything in it. It's just that he flirted with other women all the time, it was the sort of thing that could have happened.'

Burt then asked her about the day before Murfitt died. 'I had to go to London on business, I have a dress shop in Ipswich called Madame Dawn and I had to go to see a manufacturer in the West End about a gown I bought from them.'

She said she was accompanied by Mr Lewis Moore King, an independent gentleman who lived at the Greyhound pub in the neighbouring village of Flempton. They got to the dress firm just before midday. Mr King had done some shopping at Robinson and Cleaver in Regent Street and at Burberry's.

They stopped for tea on the way back and arrived back in Fornham at around 7.30. After they had finished the interviews Burt and Spooner drove to the Greyhound pub to see Lewis King, who confirmed what Elaine Browne had told them about the day in London.

Burt still thought Charlie Browne must have known something about his wife's affair but knew it would be difficult to prove it. Also he suspected Mrs Browne and Murfitt has carried on with their affair and that she was making accusations about his niece to try to stir up trouble between the Murfitts, but on the evidence so far it seemed unlikely that either of the Brownes could have put the cyanide in Murfitt's salts.

• •

When they got back to the hotel Spooner told Burt what the Murfitt's maid and chauffeur had told him the previous day about seeing a woman walking at night outside Quays Farm on two occasions before he died. They both seemed definite it was Mrs Chandler and the sergeant said he 'had a feeling' about it. Burt then spoke of one of his own pet theories that had helped him in the past. It was about the burglar who robs a shop and who, if he meets a policeman on the street corner, always stops for a chat. 'I've often wondered why he does it – conceit, super self-confidence, a queer sort of wish for human society, perhaps. It's funny how often it betrays them,' Burt said.

Spooner didn't grasp the connection until Burt reminded him of the story they had been told by the Murfitts of Mrs Chandler's visit to Quays Farm the day after Murfitt's death with the cake. Was it her way of returning to the scene of the crime? It might seem far-fetched but they did not have many leads at that stage and they had to look at all the options, Burt said. Spooner said he would make arrangements for them to see Walker and his housekeeper at Hall Farm.

Eleven   **James Walker, gentleman farmer**

Eleven

James Walker, gentleman farmer

WHEN JAMES LAING WALKER TOOK over Hall Farm in Risby in 1926 he thought it was the place he had been looking for all his life. The mellow Tudor farmhouse with its grey-slate roof was on the site of one of three ancient manors which had formed the original Saxon village. At the front it looked eastward over a meadow towards the church, at the side was another meadow for his herd of milking cows and at the back was a large garden with well-kept lawn and numerous shrubs where he could indulge his passion for unusual and exotic plants and trees.

Until he came to Risby Walker's life had been that of a wanderer. He was born in Calcutta, where his father had retired after building jute mills in India. When he travelled to Britain one of his father's contacts gave him a job in a jute mill in Edinburgh, but his real ambition was to be a farmer. When he moved south he took on a job as farm foreman at Fordham, just outside Newmarket, where he met Minnie Townsend, one of two talented sisters whose parents ran a prosperous garden and nursery business in the village. They married in 1908 and when, 18 years later, he wanted to take over Hall Farm his father put up the £1,500 capital which was needed. They looked forward to a happy and well-heeled future until, tragically, Minnie died suddenly in the June of 1926, soon after they moved in. She was only 48.

They buried her in Risby churchyard and he returned to Hall Farm determined to carry on with his new life there, in memory of Minnie he told members of her family, and his first harvest was plentiful. His workmen and domestic staff noticed, though, that he was abjectly lonely, spending long periods walking his fields or sitting in the garden in the afternoons just staring ahead as the sun went down. They were desperately sorry for him and wondered about his future.

Then six months later his employees, and people in the village, were somewhat surprised at the arrival at Hall Farm of Mrs Chandler – Mary Elizabeth Fernie Chandler, thirty at the most, with a lilting Scottish accent and a penchant for stylish clothes, fashionable hats and with a habit of sleeping in late in the mornings, which they thought strange for someone who had been introduced to them as Mr Walker's new housekeeper.

With her arrival Walker seemed happy again. He busied himself about the farm, which prospered as a result, and he left himself enough time to play golf frequently at the small but well-thought-of golf club in nearby Flempton. His social life also blossomed among the neighbouring farming community, although some eyebrows were raised when soon after she had taken up her domestic position he began to take Mrs Chandler to dinners and parties, where he introduced her to one and all as Fernie.

Walker had returned that morning from walking his spaniel in the lane outside the farm when the telephone rang and a gruff Cockney voice introduced himself at Detective Sergeant Spooner and said that he and Chief Inspector Burt would be in Risby shortly and would like to talk to him and Mrs Chandler as part of their inquiries into the death of William Murfitt.

Walker had admired Murfitt as a successful, forward-looking farmer, although he thought he treated agriculture as more of a business than some gentleman farmers, such as himself. When Murfitt had told him a month or so ago that he did not wish to entertain Fernie at Quays Farm ever again after her conduct at the card table he had been sorry. Walker did not believe there was any real harm in her. She had been forced to fight her way through life and on the way had acquired some funny little ways, but once you knew her well, as he did, then she could be captivating.

As he waited for the detectives, Walker wondered how much they wanted to talk about Murfitt's death and how much about other things. He knew that Fernie had been questioned by the local police about the fur coat she brought home after she had been to the Newmarket races with Murfitt, but from what she had told him she had a good answer for that.

Walker was standing at his living room window looking out towards the rectory, where the white candle blooms were just coming out on the horse chestnut trees which towered over the church, when the maid came in and told him two gentlemen were at the side door asking to see him.

At first Walker was very guarded in what he said about Mrs Chandler's involvement in the fur coat case, saying that he was reluctant to make a statement to the detectives without having his solicitor present, but he later agreed to do so. He had seen a barrister friend in London and intended to instruct counsel to defend her in court if the fur coat case came to court. Even is she was sent to prison, he would stand by her and would always provide a home for her, he said. Burt could tell there was a closer bond than might be thought normal between the farmer and housekeeper.

Burt began in his usual conversational style, asking what Walker had been doing just before and after Murfitt's death. Walker said that on the Monday he had been on his farm all day. In the morning he had been out in the field opposite the farm preparing it for mustard seed, returned to the farm for lunch and spent the afternoon doing various jobs about the farmyard. In the evening he did some gardening, he remembered Mrs Chandler sat out on the lawn doing some embroidery, and he had some supper before going to bed soon after ten o'clock. The next morning he got up around eight o'clock, had breakfast and went on to the farm. It was about 10.30 that he heard about Murfitt's death and the news had shaken him. He seemed such a fit man.

Burt asked how long he had lived in the village and he said since 1926. Walker told Burt of his wife's death soon after they moved in and how Mrs Chandler had joined him as housekeeper later that year.

Had he known Mrs Chandler before that? Yes, for some time, Walker said, for some 15 years or more, and she had been of great help to him in running the house. He then went on to say how the police investigation into the fur coat had been getting his housekeeper down, but she had a complete answer to the whole thing.

Burt then asked more about the fur coat case and how the Murfitts were involved in it. Walker said he and his housekeeper were very friendly with Bill and Gertie. Fernie often used to go to Newmarket with her friends and once or twice she went with Bill on her own. She loved the races. And they often used to go to Quays Farm for supper and a game of cards and so on, but they hadn't seen the Murfitts for some weeks now.'

How was that? Burt asked.

It was at the beginning of March, Walker said. Fernie thought she would like to go to see her relatives in Scotland. He drove up to see her on April 2nd, when he gave young Billy Murfitt a lift as far as Newcastle, where he was going to inquire about getting a job on a boat. He picked him up again at Newcastle when he returned three days later.

Over the Easter holiday he decided to go back up to Buck-haven, where Fernie was staying, but unfortunately he had smashed his car up so he borrowed Billy's to get as far as Peter-borough and took a train the rest of the way. Soon after he arrived, Fernie told him she had been interviewed up there by an Inspector McCallum about the theft of a fur coat. It was the first he had heard anything about it.

He brought Fernie back to Risby the following day, but before they left, Inspector McCallum advised them they should not make contact with the Murfitts, or anyone else concerned in the case, while the investigations were going on. Because of that they decided they should not visit the Murfitts again until the matter was all cleared up.

Burt and Spooner both looked surprised. They had heard from Mrs Murfitt and other at Quays Farm about Murfitt stopping the visits because of Mrs Chandler's cheating at cards.

Walker was asked 'Nothing else? You didn't have a row with them or anything?'

'Good heavens, no,' said Walker, 'we were still good friends with them.'

Burt and Spooner were to realise later that Walker had set the pattern of lying, sometimes about quite small matters, which was to cost them a lot of time in their investigations later.

Walker went on to say that when he and Mrs Chandler came back from Scotland on April 19 he returned Billy Murfitt's car to the farm and a few days later, after he had been interviewed by Inspector Butcher from Newmarket about the fur coat, he met Mrs Murfitt in a nearby lane. She told him the police had taken statements from Murfitt and herself about the coat, but she was friendly and said she and Bill were sorry over the trouble that had arisen.

Burt then asked Walker whether he had bought any cyanide recently. The farmer said he had bought a small bottle the previous September which he used to destroy wasps' and hornets' nests. Afterwards he destroyed the bottle by putting it in his slow combustion stove. No, he didn't give any of the cyanide to anyone else or allow anyone else to handle it.

He also said that when they were having meals at the Murfitts he never saw any salts there and did not know the couple took them. 'I always got on very well with Bill and I can't think of anyone with a grudge against him,' he said.

Burt then asked if they could speak to Mrs Chandler but he was told she was still in bed, and they arranged to return after lunch. She confirmed much of what Walker had said of their friendship with the Murfitts and, like Walker, refuted any suggestion that they had stopped visiting Quays Farm because they had an argument with Bill and Gertrude. They only stopped going because the inspector in Scotland warned them that it would not be wise because of the investigations going on about the fur coat, she said. She said she had been to the races with

Murfitt alone only three times. She knew he suffered from diabetes but she was not aware he ever took salts and did not know that any were kept in the dining room.

● ●

When they had a drink later that evening, Burt and Spooner discussed the interviews with Walker and Mrs Chandler. Burt said he did not think Walker was being entirely frank with them and had been careful to confine the movements of Mrs Chandler and himself to his farm and grounds on the Monday and Tuesday. He had also been careful to account conclusively for the disposal of any cyanide he had.

As for the reason they gave for stopping visits to Quays Farm, the detectives knew that Inspector McCallum in Scotland had only told Walker and Mrs Chandler not to speak to the owner of the fur coat and had not warned them about speaking to the Murfitts.

The detectives also went over what had happened as they were leaving Hall Farm. Walker and Mrs Chandler both said they knew a 'great secret' about Murfitt's life that would probably explain his death but that they could not repeat it as it would be a breach of confidence. Burt had taken Walker aside and invited him to tell him what the secret was, but although Walker worded what he said very carefully, Burt gathered he was hinting that Murfitt had committed suicide. While they were talking Spooner also asked Mrs Chandler what the secret was. She said Murfitt used to confide in her – 'He had a lot of trouble, and the truth of it is he took his own life.'

To the detectives the explanation came out too easily and had obviously been rehearsed between Walker and his house-keeper, perhaps as a way of diverting attention away from themselves. Burt knew then that he needed to know a lot more about the cagey farmer and his glamorous housekeeper and he asked Spooner to look into their backgrounds.

It was now Thursday, May 26 and nine days after Murfitt had died. Detective Chief Inspector Burt and Detective Sergeant Spooner felt that at last there was a hint of progress in their investigations.

Twelve **The sailor returns**

Twelve
The sailor returns

ALTHOUGH RISBY PEOPLE KNEW – EXPECTED – that their local newspapers, the weekly Bury Free Press and the morning East Anglian Daily Times, would cover Murfitt's death and the police investigations in detail, it came as a shock to them to discover the amount of coverage their village was getting in the Fleet Street newspapers. The first national stories appeared on the Sunday after Murfitt's death and continued during the week and the publicity burst the bubble of comfortable security in which the village had existed until then.

Ricky Murfitt had obviously been appointed the family spokesman and she was quoted in stories saying that her father-in-law was a man who didn't have an enemy in the world and who separated his home life from the farm as much as possible. Newspapers reported how Murfitt was known as the friend of roadsters, the unemployed men who walked from village in search of work and who could always get a job at Quays Farm when any of the crops were being harvested. The papers also said his employees referred to him as The Colonel, which mystified the villagers because no-one had ever remembered anyone calling him that.

The Daily Mail, whose reporter seemed to have a good rapport with Burt, gave the first hints in journalistic code of the scandal of Murfitt's private life that was emerging in a story which said that as the Yard man delved deeper into the life and death of the farmer he had learned many unexpected and puzzling facts. 'He has only been able to touch the fringe of a mystery which has excited enormous local interest and gossip,' the reporter wrote. 'He knows Mr Murfitt was a surprisingly virile man who moved in a small company of friends of both sexes in the Bury St Edmunds and Newmarket areas and some further afield.'

The Daily Express reported how Burt had worked day long at Murfitt's desk in his office studying ledgers and accounts dealing with the farmer's finances. The story also recounted how, on an evening just before his death, Murfitt was in good spirits when he had played snooker at a Newmarket club with a group of well-known jockeys and trainers who were his close friends, and with whom he had formed a syndicate to rent a 1,200 acre shoot near Thetford.

The drama in the small Suffolk village was played out to the background of the major, long-running international news stories of the time – the latest atrocities in the Spanish Civil War, German troops massing on the Czechoslovakian border and Japanese troops invading China.

One edition of the Daily Express told how Burt and Spooner had interviewed Mrs Murfitt at the farm at the weekend, a news story it rated so highly that it gave it shared prominence on Page One with a declaration by its proprietor, Lord Beaver-brook, about the worsening situation in Europe. He wrote: 'Britain will not be involved in war. There will be no major war in Europe either this year or next year. The Germans will not seize Czechoslovakia, so go about your own business with confidence and fear not. Provide us with airplanes, anti-aircraft guns and ammunition and develop our own Imperial resources and give us greater prosperity and happiness at home.' Like so many predictions at that time, it was not to come true.

The News of the World gave space to an article by the rebellious MP Winston Churchill under the headline 'Why Not the United States of Europe. Away With the Barriers Which Divide our Common Interest.' Other news stories told how every area in Britain was to have fire-fighting services for all purposes of war and peace, including dealing with incendiary bombs, and readers were told of the formation of barrage balloon units to keep enemy bombers from our towns and cities. Suffolk was used for Britain to show off its increasing air strength, perhaps as a warning to others, and the skies were full of noise as Mildenhall and Stradishall aerodromes put on displays for Empire Air Day, when 400 airplanes, including the latest bombers the Handley-Page Harrows and the Heyfords, took to the air.

For the newspapers, the investigation in Risby by Burt and Spooner had all the essential ingredients of a successful book – a mysterious death by poison, adulterous sex in privileged circles, the arrival of two of the country's up-and-coming detectives from Scotland Yard, the mention of well-known names from the Newmarket racing set, all set amid a tranquil countryside in the best manner of Agatha Christie whose works were at that time entertaining the expanding market of readers of detective novels. The invasion of reporters and cameramen brought a boom to local hotels, whose prices inevitably went up as the normal clientele of commercial travellers and the occasional tourist found it harder to secure a vacant room in an area 20 miles around Bury St Edmunds.

Burt and Spooner didn't mind the newspapers' attention. It was part of being in the Murder Squad and they knew, without ever mentioning it, that it would do no harm to their future careers. They both had their own close contacts among the

Fleet Street crime reporters whom they could use to help further their investigations, trading in return exclusive tip-offs and news angles. After one hard day of interviews in the village the two detectives sat over a quiet drink in Burt's hotel room and the question of newspaper coverage came up. There had been a few sharp comments from the West Suffolk police, whose policy was usually to say as little as possible, that it all seemed to be getting out of hand. 'Unseemly,' was the word used by one of the Chief Constable's senior officers.

• •

Over the years urban myths have grown up in the closely-knit worlds of policemen and journalists about investigations and their coverage. I heard one of these in a Fleet Street pub in the 1950s, told as if it had only just happened. A gnarled and experienced journalist grunted sceptically, 'That's a coincidence, I heard much the same story just before the war.' If it happened then, I like to think it might have been during the Murfitt case. The story concerns a party which the crime reporters gave in a hotel bar for the police as a way to foster better relations, and the celebrations went on into the early hours of the morning. As in Bury St Edmunds, the hotels were crowded and many people had to share rooms, most of which at that time did not have en-suite bathrooms. One photographer, a non drinker, retired to bed early only to be awakened at about 3am by his reporter bursting into the room, switching on the light and after unbuttoning his flies relieving himself in the washbasin. The photographer, short in stature and normally mild-mannered, jumped out of bed and screaming obscenities gave the reporter a couple of right-handers to the jaw. The photographer stag-

gered back, astounded. 'What's wrong, matey,' he asked. 'You
bastard,' the photographer shouted back, 'my teeth are in there.'

• •

When the captain of the SS Baron Murray received a radio message as the ship sailed through the Mediterranean he called young Billy Murfitt, his fourth engineer, to his cabin to tell him the sad news of his father's sudden death. That message, as a result of Mollie Targett's' telephone call to the shipping agents on the day Murfitt died, was followed shortly after by another radio message, this time from Scotland Yard, telling the captain they wanted Billy to return home immediately.

The captain was sympathetic but the police message faced him with his own problems. Billy shared the three daily eight-hour shifts with two other engineers and his leaving would mean the other two would now have to work twelve-hour shifts until the end of the journey. An unscheduled stop to put Billy off at the nearest port would cause the ship an inconvenient delay, and time was money.

In the end the captain turned the Baron Murray towards the Italian coast and landed at Genoa, where Billy was paid off and took a train to Milan. He could sense a strange mood among his fellow passengers, a mixture of excitement and apprehension. He realised later that it was caused by the recent visit to Rome by the German Fuhrer Adolf Hitler to meet Mussolini to ensure the Italian dictator's support for his future ambitions in Europe.

Billy's intention was to catch the express train to Paris but, because of Mussolini's recently announced mobilisation plans, there were queues at all the railway stations and he had to spend most of the cash he had on him on an air ticket to the French capital, where he spent the rest of his money on a rail and ferry ticket to London. On May 28, eleven days after his father's death, he arrived back at Quays Farm, tired and distraught, to be met in the hallway of the farmhouse by his mother, who collapsed weeping in his arms. He led her into the lounge where, piece-by-piece, she told him how his father had died, of the police investigations and of her questioning by the Scotland Yard detectives, particularly by 'that bloody Spooner'.

The police had left a request for Billy to telephone them on his return, which he did, and Burt and Spooner arrived at Quays Farm shortly afterwards. Burt expressed his sympathy to Billy over his father's death while Spooner got out his notebook and stared straight at him without saying a word. Billy could under-stand his mother's reaction to the man. Burt struck up a friendly conversation, starting with Billy's journey home from the Mediterranean, laughing quietly with him at the scenes he wit-nessed in Italy, and then gradually moving on to Billy's earlier life and how he had worked with his father on his farms from the time he left school. Billy said he was proud of what his father had done and as he was keen on cars and engineering himself he had been pleased to see the latest tractors and other equipment being used on the farm, and he had enjoyed driving the lorries to London and back. Billy had ideas of his own of how the business could grow faster and this eventually brought him into conflict with his father, who thought he was interfering too much. As a result, Billy said, just over three years ago he went off to Wisbech to work for a potato merchant, but he returned six months later when his father offered him an increase in wages after his mother asked Murfitt to make his son welcome back home.

They did have a row about 18 months ago when he thought his father was unduly familiar with Elaine Browne and he told him so. Murfitt told his son to mind his own business and rather than let his mother know about the argument he decided to drop the matter.

Spooner said he had heard stories in the village that Billy still did not get on with his father and they had been heard arguing. Did he have anything against him? Billy said he had no quarrel with his father at the time he left to go to sea. He was furious because he could sense Spooner was trying to insinuate he might have had something to do with his father's death.

William Murfitt, a studio photograph

Thirteen **Beer runs out at the auction**

Thirteen

Beer runs out at the auction

WITH BILLY MURFITT'S RETURN TO RISBY, as well as having to come to terms with the death of his father he was immediately thrown into discussions about the family's future. Although he would have liked to take over Quays Farm he knew he didn't have the money behind him to do so. Like many a 25-year-old he had not thought yet about saving, and a liking for girls and fast cars had taken most of the money he earned. Also, his ambition to get his Flying Flea, a kit aeroplane he was building in the workshop at the farm, into the air had also taken more money and time.

His brother Leslie had his motor business in London and had never had ambitions to be a farmer and their mother was still alternating between acute depression and, Burt had noted, a strange, almost detached attitude to her situation, as though she could still not believe her husband was dead, and was in no state to make major decisions.

Although Murfitt was still being referred to in the national newspapers as a wealthy farmer, the description was not borne out when the boys came to look at the business and family finances. There was no doubt that he had been making good money at Quays Farm, with net profits of nearly £3,500 for the year ending May 1937 and between £5,000 and £6,000 for the year up to his death. Just before he died, when his accountants did a statement for the bank in support of an application for an overdraft for business expansion, they calculated he had a surplus of nearly £11,500 – this at a time when a small farm with 15 acres and a house was being advertised in a neighbouring village for £1,000.

But Murfitt's business, and his lifestyle, needed to be lubricated by large sums of money. He had spent heavily on the most modern farm machinery and on improving his buildings, which enhanced his prospects for the future, but which needed a good cashflow to sustain for the present. His wage bill was high because he believed in paying well to get his crops to the market quickly and efficiently, the family lived well and, with his interests in large cars, shooting parties, and horseracing, his personal expenses were higher than most of his neighbouring farmers.

Gertrude had already given him a loan of £1,600 from her own money and had guaranteed his overdrafts to the tune of £4,000. In fact, when Burt looked into the family accounts to see if there could have been a financial motive for her to kill her husband he came to the conclusion it would not have been worth her while, although he still had not finally dismissed the possibility that she had done it out of jealousy. Burt had also heard of gossip among the local farming community that Murfitt had been in financial difficulties and as a result had committed suicide, but this turned out to be completely untrue.

After a long discussion the family decided their only option was to sell up and realise the cash and within days, valuers from the local auctioneers Lacy Scott and Sons were going round the farm with clipboards putting a price on everything, from the Carrimore lorries to Murfitt's gundogs and their kennels. Jim Pryke, proudly driving one of Murfitt's two huge tracked tractors with a set of rollers wider than anyone in Suffolk had seen before, was stopped halfway across a field while a valuer climbed over the machine to try to estimate how much it would fetch. With his wry countryman's humour Jim told the young man, 'You can count me in as well, if you like. I don't reckon there's many people can drive one of these, so I must be worth a quid or two.'

The auctioneers' advertisement appeared in local newspapers the following weekend announcing the sale on Thursday June 9th – 'One of the biggest agricultural sales held in the district,' it said in the editorial columns. Prospective buyers were enticed by the list, including 50 Angus Cross and Shorthorn cattle, many suitable for Christmas Show purposes, 220 Essex, Large Black and Large White pigs, 228 Black-Faced and Dorset Horn ewes and lambs and 300 head of poultry. Farmers who had envied Murfitt's growing stock of machines, 'many nearly new as adapted for large-scale mechanical farming,' said the advertisement, were excited by the news that they would be able to bid for the two 44 horse-power Lanz Crawler tractors, five-furrow ploughs and harrows up to 32-feet wide. The catalogue listed more than 100 lots.

On the day of the auction people started arriving before breakfast so that they could inspect the lots before the sale began at 10.30am. PC Carrington took up his post at the farm gate to direct cars to the allocated parking areas, which were soon full. Many people arrived on the train at Saxham and Risby station and walked across the bridle path leading to the farm. Families of gypsies, some of whom had arrived two or three days before, to the consternation of the Risby villagers, went round looking at the horses and the smaller pieces of equipment and PC Carrington asked Syd Williams to detail some of his men to watch them to make sure all the lots were still there when the time came for them to go under the hammer.

When the auction began 1,500 people, some from as far afield as Cumberland and Sussex, thronged the sales area at the back of the farm and 500 cars filled the parking areas, lined the grass verges throughout the village and covered large areas of the two village greens. A large marquee set up for refreshments had a queue waiting outside when it opened and by lunchtime the auctioneers had to send down to Greene King's brewery in Bury St Edmunds for extra supplies. Burt and Spooner did not attend but the local police were out in force. The reporters were there, those from the local papers noting down every individual price paid while those from the national papers were looking for what they called a 'colour story,' much of which was mutually agreed among them inside the beer tent. Billy and Leslie Murfitt walked sadly among the crowd while the rest of the Murfitt family and some of their friends, stayed indoors.

The Angus steers and heifers fetched prices well over the valuers' estimates and there was a big demand for the pigs and poultry. One of Murfitt's favourite gun-trained springer spaniels, shivering with fright and looking sad, brought tears to the eyes of women in the crowd as it was knocked down for ten guineas and there were more tears as its month-old puppies fetched four guineas each. A pair of Murfitt's prized Churchill 12-bore shotguns with extra sets of barrels were bought for £125 by a member of the shooting syndicate he was forming, and another pair of 12-bores fetched £70.

The year-old black Buick which had identified Murfitt as he drove around West Suffolk went for £375 and the family's other car, a Ford Eight, was sold for £72.10s. The two crawler tractors were sold for £280 and £200, and an ageing lorry for £10. A three-speed cycle with the latest dynamo lighting went for £5 12s 6d and Murfitt's billiards table for £8. Billy Murfitt stood disconsolately at the back of the bidders in the workshed as his beloved Flying Flea, in which he had just mounted a new Douglas engine, went under the hammer for a wretched £5. 'I never even got the chance to fly it,' he said as he walked away. 'Just as well,' said one of his young friends, 'they haven't got a very good flying record.'

The sale lasted until teatime and raised well over £1,000. By the end of the day many of the visitors were feeling somewhat the worse for wear as a result of their steady intake throughout the day of Greene King's India Pale Ale. Many declared the day better than the Suffolk Show, which had been ruined by torrential rain and heavy winds the week before.

Mrs Murfitt, a sad little figure as she sat on her own in the dining room, could see the crowds as they trailed out of the farm's main gateway, meeting on the way the lorries and carts coming in to collect the sold items for their new owners. She had been so full of hope when she and Bill first arrived to look over Quays Farm but now it had come to this, so quickly – it was just over three weeks since her husband had died and now all their possessions, apart from their household effects, were in the hands of others. Even worse, the disgrace that Bill had brought on the family through his affairs with other women was now known to the police and would no doubt soon be common knowledge.

Fourteen   **A bottle marked poison**

Fourteen
A bottle marked poison

AFTER THE DETECTIVES' INTERVIEWS WITH Walker and Mrs Chandler, Reg Spooner set about getting a full background on the pair with the assistance of police in London and Scotland. Burt, meanwhile, asked the West Suffolk Chief Constable Colin Robertson for help in carrying out tests into how cyanide interacted with Fynnon Salts and to widen the search for sales of the poison, as the local investigation had been inconclusive. As a result policemen more used to dealing with traffic offences and petty crime spent several hours in the police station mixing the health salts with the poison and observing the results.

They discovered that when the two substances were mixed they set up a chemical reaction which produced dampness and discolouration, such as Mrs Murfitt found in the packet from which she gave her husband his last dose. They also found that the longer the mixture was left the more it would congeal into a damp, dark brown lump giving off a pungent odour, and the degree of dampness, discolouration and smell could show how long the poison had been in the salts. When he went to London, Burt called again at St Mary's Hospital in Paddington and asked Roche Lynch, the Home Office analyst, to carry out some tests of his own along these lines with cyanide bought or found in Bury St Edmunds or Risby. The analyst said the results of his tests showed that when Mrs Murfitt opened the tin of Fynnon Salts on May 17 there would have been about ten grains of cyanide in the salts – about twice a minimum lethal dose – and that they would have been placed there some time between the previous evening and 6 o'clock on the morning of Murfitt's death.

The earlier search among West Suffolk chemists' records had failed to show any recent sales of cyanide which could have had a bearing on the farmer's death and it was decided to extend the search nationally, bearing in mind that the Murfitts, Walker, Mrs Chandler and Mrs Browne had travelled extensively by car to places such as London and Scotland. A notice was published in the Police Gazette and Metropolitan Police Information asking that all Poison Registers be searched to see if any cyanide had been bought during the past six months which could be traced to anyone living in West Suffolk. Dozens of policemen in Forces throughout England, Scotland and Wales were sent out to search the documents of their local chemists, but they were unable to discover if any such purchases had been made.

At the same time all foodstuffs in Quays Farm were examined to see if they had been tampered with and Dr Roche Lynch was surprised to receive a parcel containing a cake, the one Mrs Chandler had delivered to the farmhouse on the day after Murfitt's death, with a request that it be tested for cyanide. He reported there were no traces of poison.

• •

Burt's suspicions that Walker and Mrs Chandler had been lying at the first interview were confirmed when he and Spooner went back to question the farmer's employees, and it was out of these inquiries that they were faced with the mystery of the dark green bottle. A maid, Violet Middleditch, who had since gone to work for another employer, recalled that the previous August Mrs Chandler went to Scotland for about six weeks. While she was away she sent the maid a letter asking her to forward a bottle which she would find in the left-hand corner of a bench in the cloakroom. The maid assumed that it must have been some sort of medicine that the sickly housekeeper had been taking but the bottle she found was labelled 'Poison' and 'Cyanide of Potassium'. The maid showed the letter and the bottle to the milk boy, Will Ashman, and they both agreed it could not be the bottle Mrs Chandler had asked for, so Miss Middleditch wrote and told the housekeeper that she could not find what she wanted. She received a reply from Mrs Chandler thanking her and saying she would get Mr Walker to deal with it.

Miss Middleditch said she had seen the dark green ridged bottle in the house previously, it contained small white lumps, was about five inches tall and carried a Boots the Chemist label. When Mrs Chandler returned in September she showed the maid the bottle labelled 'Cyanide of Potassium' and said that was the one she had asked for. It was to destroy some wasps nests in Scotland and it was difficult to buy the poison there, she said. The maid's story was confirmed by young Will Ashman.

The detectives also spoke to Jack Turner, Walker's foreman at the time, who said that in July the previous year Walker gave him a bottle of cyanide to destroy a wasps nest on the farm and he used the same bottle to destroy two more nests towards the end of August.

Later the milk boy, Will Ashman, said he now recalled that on September 17 – he remembered the date because he started his holidays the day after – Walker gave him a small bottle with some cyanide in to destroy a wasps' nest near his cottage. He used all of the poison and disposed of the bottle by putting it in the hollow of the tree where the nest was.

The detectives saw Walker again and repeated the questions about buying and using cyanide they had put to him at the first interview. He insisted that he only bought one bottle of the poison in September, used it himself to destroy a hornets' nest and two wasps' nests and a few days later destroyed the bottle by putting it in the slow combustion stove. No-one else had access to it, he repeated. When the detectives saw Mrs Chandler later that day she confirmed exactly what Walker had said, adding her own description, 'The fire melted the glass and it came out just like a clinker.'

Burt and Spooner noted that the couple reeled off these answers as if they had rehearsed them first. The fact that other people on the farm had used cyanide, or that a bottle of it was lying around the house, wasn't proof that they used it on Murfitt, but they seem to be lying for the sake of it. Why?

What annoyed Burt more than anything else was that checking and rechecking the stories of Walker and his housekeeper was taking up valuable time which he could ill afford to spare. He still had to return to the Yard from time-to-time to deal with some of his previous cases and it was delaying his investigation into the Risby murder. He had heard from the Chief Constable that the Coroner was starting to ask how the inquiry was going, whether there would be any charges made or whether he should start to prepare for the inquest, which he had formally opened and adjourned two days after Murfitt's death, to be resumed.

Burt decided to arrange another meeting with Walker and Chandler and when the detectives called at Hall Farm they were surprised to be introduced to a Mr Bateman, Walker's solicitor, from London. Burt started with a question to the housekeeper – did she remember writing to the maid asking for a bottle to be sent to her in Scotland? Mrs Chandler agreed that she had done so. What had she wanted it for? She replied, 'Lotion'. Burt told her that didn't coincide with what the maid had said, would she prepared to put her replies from now on in a written statement?

The solicitor protested and asked to confer with his client. They went to an adjoining room, where they talked with Walker, and returned to say Mrs Chandler was now willing to make a written statement. The housekeeper then said the bottle she had written to the maid about contained boracic crystals. After the maid wrote that she could not find it she wrote to Walker to ask him to send it, but he could not find it either.

Spooner asked why she wanted boracic crystals sent through the post. They could be bought in any chemists for two or three pence, and they came in packets, not bottles. Mrs Chandler said the bottle she wanted contained boracic crystals. She could not remember having a conversation with Miss Middleditch about the matter when she returned from Scotland. The maid must have it wrong.

Burt then called Walker in and questioned him about his purchases and use of cyanide. Walker now changed his story. He had inquired at Boots, he said, and it appeared he had bought cyanide in August 1934, November 1936, September 1936 and the last on July 19th 1937. He now remembered giving some to the foreman Jack Turner, who had returned the bottle to him. He gave the same bottle to Will Ashman and told him if he used all the poison to make sure he destroyed the bottle.

When Spooner recalled his previous statement Walker apologised and said he remembered more about it now. Had he been talking to his employees about the matter, he was asked. The solicitor said he did not think that was a relevant question and told Walker not to answer.

Burt then asked him about Mrs Chandler's request from Scotland asking for the bottle to be sent to her and the farmer seemed to develop a loss of memory about the whole matter. Yes, she had written asking him to send her something, but he could not remember what it was. No, he could not remember her asking him to send a bottle of cyanide and he did not do so, as far as he could remember.

Burt glanced at Walker, who now lay almost horizontal on an armchair with his eyes closed and his head thrown back, had become very nervous and was obviously in considerable mental distress. He was being over-cautious about his replies and saying over and over again that he could not remember. The solicitor suggested the interview should end and Burt and Spooner left, frustrated.

Fifteen **The lady with a past**

Fifteen
The lady with a past

The information on the life and background of Mrs Chandler, which Burt received, showed a woman with a lowly beginning and wayward youth who tried to better herself, but who then fell into a life of lying, deception, petty thieving and fantasy. Her adventures among her friends in the Bury St Edmunds area made the detective comment in his report that she was 'the type of person who would experience little difficulty in gaining access to other people's houses unnoticed'. He remarked on 'the effron-tery of this woman' and on her apparent spiteful and vicious nature. None of this information could be disclosed at the time, either in the newspapers or in the later legal hearings, but Burt now considered her a major suspect in the search for Bill Murfitt's poisoner.

MARY ELIZABETH FERNIE HIGGINS WAS born at Pitlessie, Fifeshire, on June 17, 1897, the daughter of a coal miner. She left school at 14 and her first job was as a pithead worker at a local colliery but after a few months she went into domestic service with a Mrs Scrymgeour-Wedderburn just outside Dundee and later with the Shiells family of Carnie, near Aberdeen. In July 1914 she was in service with the Reckie family in Kirkaldy, where she stayed for the duration of the war, but when her employers were packing up to move house in 1918 Mrs Reckie discovered a parcel of clothes and other articles were missing. Young Mary Higgins was challenged and she admitted theft when the parcel was found in her trunk. She was dismissed, but that was not the last the family saw of her. Two years later Mr Reckie was surprised to receive an account from an Edinburgh firm of ladies' outfitters for goods supplied. He returned the account denying any knowledge of the purchases and when the police were called in they traced the order to Mary Higgins, who by then was 23, was working as a nurse and had acquired a taste for clothes which she could not always afford.

The case, however, never came to court. When the Reckie family learned that Mary had secured a job as a nurse-governess with the family of Lord Beckenham, who was about to leave for India, they asked the police to drop the charge. Life among colonial society of the sub-continent obviously suited the girl from the pit village and in 1922 she married Joseph Henry Chandler, a wealthy widower who owned chemists shops in two Indian towns. She mixed with the British Raj society, living in large houses with numerous servants and plenty of money paid into her own account by a devoted husband. The only problem was that Mr Chandler had a teenage daughter to whom Mary took a violent dislike and in 1924 she left India to sail to England.

Her husband made sure she had a reasonable sum in her bank account to see her through and sent her some more when she was in London. He was saddened and surprised to receive a letter from his wife asking for more money to enable her to have an operation for a blood clot on the brain and he sent her another £50, only to discover later that she never had the operation.

It was 1924, London's bright young things were livening up the West End with cocktails parties and wild dances like the Charleston and the Black Bottom and prominent among them was a stylish young woman of 27 who, depending on which set of friends she was with, was known as Lady Fernie or Lady Mary. She talked of the grand life she had lived in India with her many servants, and she casually dropped the names of the famous and the infamous she had met in her exciting life. Her new-found friends were a little surprised when she kept changing her address from one hotel to another, then one day she said she was going to visit her relatives in Scotland and they heard no more of her.

• •

The police trail followed Fernie Chandler to Risby, where she came to the attention of a Commission Agent, or bookmaker, Frederick Turvey, whom she chose as her unlikely victim in a betting scam she devised in such a way to make sure she couldn't lose. Mr Turvey was happy to accept bets placed with him in telephone calls which he understood to come from various wives of men well-known in the area, and the book-maker sometimes wondered if their husbands knew of their habit of having a flutter.

One client said she was Mrs Gittus, of Barrow, and the book-maker knew her husband was a successful breeder of pedigree pigs. Mrs Browne he knew as a farmer's wife from Fornham All Saints and Mrs Plumpton was a businessman's wife from Bury. At first Mr Turvey had no suspicions about the origins of the bets and when Mrs Browne's horse won he happily paid the lady with the Scottish accent who called at his office the winnings of £4 11s 4d, the equivalent of a two week's pay for many people. When the £6 bets placed on their fancies by Mrs Gittus and Mrs Plumpton did not win he sent their accounts to their home addresses, in plain envelopes of course, and he was somewhat angry when they both replied that they had not made the bets at all. Because of the nature of his business – as a commission agent you did not always want to draw the attention of the authorities to yourself unless really necessary – he let the matter lie.

Sometime later, on a Saturday lunchtime, a Mrs Seth, of Bury St Edmunds, rang the bookmaker to place the sizeable stake of £12 on one of the afternoon's runners. Mr Turvey got one of his assistants to check the call and, on finding it was being made from a telephone box in Bury, he refused to accept the bet. Within a few minutes Mrs Chandler appeared in his office and the bookmaker's son recognised the Scottish accent which had made the call in the name of Mrs Seth. When the matter of the £12 bet was taken up with her she was most indignant. 'Surely you are not accusing me of that,' she said. 'I have a perfect alibi,' omitting to say that on her way home she intended to call at her hairdressers to try to persuade an assistant, just in case anyone asked, that she was there an hour before she actually was.

Quays Farm in 1938. The theory is the poisoner went in by the
front door and into the dining room immediately on the right

Mrs Chandler must have told Walker about her troubles because a few days later he called on Mr Turvey and begged him not to prosecute her. The bookmaker agreed Walker could pay him £40 for the money he had lost through Fernie's fraudulent scheme and accepted £10 on the spot, although so far only £5 had been paid off the balance of the debt.

Fernie Chandler also had unusual shopping habits, such as the time she called into a grocer's in the town centre and ordered a basket-load of supplies, asking for the bill to be put on Mrs Browne's account. She then pointed to 'her' car in the market square and asked the shop assistant to place the groceries in it while she continued shopping. When the real owner of the car arrived he was approached by a lady with a Scottish accent who said her goods had been put in his car by mistake, and she collected them from him and walked away. When the police investigated they had one clue, that among the goods were some sweets identical to sweets which Mrs Chandler later gave to her friend Gertrude Murfitt, but they did not think they had enough evidence for a prosecution.

Burt was slightly amused by the audacity and resourcefulness shown in crimes so far, but he lost any sympathy when he read on, about the activities of a common thief. One example was the theft of a lady's handbag from a Bury cafe which Mrs Chandler had visited, following which Walker took a cigarette case to the police station saying she had found it in the street. It was the same cigarette case which had been in the handbag when it was stolen. On other occasions Mrs Chandler was seen with a new crocodile handbag very much like the one missing from a jewellers' shop, and after several petty thefts at Flempton Golf Club, where Walker played, she was the leading suspect even though no-one could prove anything.

Walker and Mrs Chandler became friendly enough with a Mr and Mrs Berry to enable them to ring the bell and walk straight upstairs to their flat in Abbeygate Street, Bury St Edmunds. The friendship cooled when they missed a £1 note from a handbag and a pair of stockings after a visit from Mrs Chandler. On another occasion, when Elaine Browne had been out with Mrs Chandler and other friends in her car she found an evening dress missing when she got home. There were other suspicions of a similar nature, not serious but difficult to prove.

It was another aspect of her character, however, that stirred Burt's interest more. Fernie Chandler, he discovered, had a reputation for being in places that she was not expected, usually somewhere in other people's homes. One day Walker and Mrs Chandler went with Gertrude to visit her sister Emma Ruston at Wisbech. The housekeeper made an excuse to go to the bathroom and after a while Mrs Murfitt went to look for her and found Mrs Chandler in her sister's bedroom, near the wardrobe. Her excuse was that she had a ladder in her stocking and was looking for a needle and cotton to mend it. Mrs Ruston later found a nightdress missing from her room. It was at the same house, on another evening, when a friend of the Rustons found a £5 note missing from her handbag, which was in the dining room where Mrs Chandler had been left alone for a time. When her friends the Berrys were interviewed about the thefts at their flat they remembered how on one visit Mrs Chandler went missing and was found at Mr Berry's desk. She made the excuse that she just wanted to write a letter.

But Burt was most interested in two stories related by Mrs Murfitt about Mrs Chandler's strange behaviour at Quays Farm. One day Gertrude was resting on her bed when there was a tap at the bedroom door and Mrs Chandler, who had gained entry to the house without being seen, walked in uninvited. 'Sorry, Gertrude, I rang the bell and couldn't make the maids hear,' she said, nonplussed. 'I've got the car outside and wondered if you would like to come up town with me.' Mrs Murfitt didn't think too much about it until another night, when Walker was at Quays Farm for supper with his house-keeper, who made an excuse to go to the bathroom. She was a long time gone and when Mrs Murfitt went to look for her she found her in the bedroom, standing quietly against the wardrobe. She said she had rung the bathroom bell for one of the maids to render her some personal service but no-one had answered. Mrs Murfitt was mystified because she knew the bell battery had just been recharged. And she wondered why Mrs Chandler needed to go into her bedroom at all.

. . . .

Leonard Burt, who liked to try to analyse what went on in the minds of his suspects, was fascinated as to why Mrs Chandler had to invent stories about herself to friends and acquaintances. He recalled Mrs Murfitt telling him that Mrs Chandler described her father as a retired barrister and that her husband was a doctor in India who died on the polo field. She let it drop casually that her husband had entertained the Prince of Wales, that she had been presented at court, that she knew Jack Buchanan the theatrical star, that she had a lot of money invested in a bank in London and had no need to touch it, and that she had a bungalow let to two doctors in India. Mrs Murfitt had said at the time she wondered why Mrs Chandler was working as a housekeeper.

Violet Middleditch, in the course of relating the story of the mysterious green bottle of poison at Hall Farm, had said Mrs Chandler had told her that her husband was a doctor living abroad, that her brother was studying to be a doctor and that her grandfather was the Earl Marshal of Scotland. She said she had attended the Coronation of King George VI in London and that when the Duke of Norfolk died her father would become Earl Marshal of England and be responsible for organising any coronations in the future. On Mr Walker's sitting room mantlepiece she kept a photograph of herself in fine clothes which she said was her court dress for royal occasions.

Even Fernie Chandler's family were not spared the fantasies. Her uncle John Higgins, an antiques dealer in Anstruther, told Scottish police that when his niece visited him in the summer of 1937 she told him, and others, that she met her husband Jim Walker when he was a doctor in India but he was now retired. His real name was Chandler but he had to change it to Walker as one of the stipulations of a family inheritance. She also told them she was a journalist and did a lot of writing for newspapers.

To the unfortunate Berry family in Bury St Edmunds she repeated the story that her father was a barrister, with a smattering of truth that his name was Higgins and that he lived in Scotland, and that on a health cruise to India she married a retired Colonel of the Indian Medical Service and repeated the tale that he died playing polo. As a by-the-way, she told them she had a motor-car in India but that it was now wrapped up in boxes, apparently awaiting transportation. The Berrys eventually became fed up with her fairy tales and concluded that she was an unmitigated liar.

Burt and Spooner knew they now had a suspect who could get in the Murfitt's house without being seen and who knew her way about it like the back of her hand. But that did not necessarily make her a poisoner and if they were to prove that, they knew they had to find out what her motive was for murder.

Sixteen **Unwanted filly that became a star**

Sixteen
Unwanted filly that became a star

Inquiries about a fur coat missing from the bedroom of the wife of leading Newmarket trainer Dawson Waugh had been continuing at the same time as the Murfitt murder inquiries. It resulted in Mrs Chandler being summoned on June 8 with stealing or receiving a mink, the property of Mrs Edith Waugh. In my research I contacted members of the Waugh family still living in Newmarket who put me in touch with Mrs Peggy Otter, Edith Waugh's daughter. I travelled to Dorset to meet her and found that, even in her 90s, she still had a sharp recollection of the case and had a lovely story to tell how her mother came to acquire the coat that later went missing.

It was partly pity and partly a hunch that made Edith Waugh bid for the little dark brown yearling as it was led around the ring. Edith had gone to the sales with her husband Dawson, a trainer who was looking for a potential Derby winner for one of his owners, but he was decidedly uninterested in the little filly. Neither were any of the other trainers and owners at Doncaster that afternoon, perhaps because of the effects of the good lunch they had just had. Edith Waugh, however, was impressed by the way the filly walked proud and held its head high and just as the bidding stopped she nodded to the auctioneer and the yearling was hers for a hundred guineas.

Dawson Waugh smiled tolerantly. As a man born into a Newmarket racing dynasty, and who had trained the 1912 Derby winner Tagalie some 20 years beforehand, he had a right to think the filly wouldn't come to much, but nevertheless he was pleased to see his wife had the courage of her convictions, even if she was wasting her own money. When they got the filly back to their headquarters at Somerville Lodge, on the edge of Newmarket, it seemed at first that he was right and that her name, Mark Time – she was by Black Watch out of Little Mark – would be particularly apt. But Edith Waugh's sympathy and hunch paid off and by the beginning of her second year the filly, with of course Dawson Waugh's expert training, was showing a good turn of speed and starting to win races. By the end of that year she was the best two-year-old in the country and after another successful season she was sold as a brood mare to Miss Dorothy Paget at a considerable profit to its owner.

There was great celebration in the Dawson Waugh household. Their two daughters, Marjory and Peggy, told their mother that, instead of spoiling them as she normally did when she had money to spend, she should buy herself a present. As a result, one October day in 1935, Edith Waugh caught the train to London, took a taxi to Mr Charles Woolf's furrier's shop in Argyle Street and for 175 guineas treated herself to a Canadian mink, one of only 12 the furrier made in a year.

When she was not wearing it to the races and at social functions with her husband the mink hung in her wardrobe, and she showed it to her many visitors as a proud memento of her ability to pick a winner. Two of her visitors who were shown the coat, in the January of 1937, were her brother-in-law Jimmy Walker, from Risby and Fernie Chandler. Edith was always pleased to see Jimmy, who had married her sister Minnie, whose sudden death in 1926 had caused the whole family to grieve. She was not certain what to make of Mrs Chandler, the housekeeper he had taken on only months after his wife's death.

Later that year, on September 29, just after Newmarket's first October meeting had begun, Edith Waugh realised the mink was missing from her wardrobe. She knew it had been there the night before, she told the police when she telephoned them in a high state of distress, and the thief would hardly have had time to get rid of it. What, she asked, were they going to do about it? Over the ensuing months the police were to learn that the wife of Dawson Waugh did not suffer fools gladly.

The 20 men in Dawson Waugh's stables next to the house were interviewed by the police and the only possible clue came from Beckett the tack man, who noticed a car near the gate when he went out to feed the pigs on the afternoon of the 29th while the Dawson Waughs were at the races. Mrs Waugh's three servants, who were in the kitchen at the back of the house, said they had not seen anyone entering or leaving the house during that time. The police were at a loss to know where to look for the thief or thieves and the investigation was not helped by Mrs Waugh's attitude that they were not doing enough. At one point Superintendent Hammond felt he had to report that owing to the victim's temperament he thought it unwise to approach her on occasions, which hampered his inquiries somewhat. Although sad at losing her coat of happy memories, Mrs Dawson Waugh approached her insurance company and although she was only covered for £100 for any one item she was satisfied when, presumably because of the other business the stables put their way, the insurers paid her £150 for her loss. The matter, she thought, was closed.

. . . .

A few weeks after the theft Mrs Murfitt made a social call on Mrs Chandler at Risby Hall Farm – the families were on good terms at the time – and found her bubbling with enthusiasm. 'Gertrude dear, come upstairs and I'll show you something fabulous,' she said, and opening her wardrobe showed Gertrude a beautiful mink coat, which she said she had been asked to sell for a friend in Scotland. Mrs Murfitt asked her why she didn't keep it for herself. Mrs Chandler said it was a little heavy for her and she preferred something lighter in weight.

When the two women met some days later Mrs Murfitt asked if she had sold the coat. Mrs Chandler said she had actually bought it herself since they last met and asked if Gertrude knew anyone who might like to buy it off her.

Mrs Murfitt suggested her own furrier, Ralli's of Regent Street, might he interest in buying it and when she next went up to London Mrs Chandler went with her and the proprietor of Ralli's said yes, he would like to see the coat. Just before Christmas Mrs Chandler and James Walker drove to Bishops Stortford station – where Walker walked proudly up and down the platform with the mink over his arm -and caught the train to London. They took the coat to Ralli's where they paid her £100 for it and in exchange she bought an ermine coat from the shop for 85 guineas.

Fur coats are not bought and sold every day in Risby and Mrs Chandler's mink became a topic of conversation between Gertrude Murfitt and Elaine Browne, who wondered, with a knowing smile, how Mrs Chandler could afford a fur coat on a housekeeper's wages. Mrs Browne, being in the fashion business, also remembered hearing about the theft of a mink from Newmarket and, began to have suspicions. These she mentioned to her husband, who mentioned them to the Bury police. Neither of them particularly liked Fernie Chandler.

The information was passed to Newmarket police who made their own inquiries and on April 11, 1938, two policemen went to Regent Street, called on Ralli Furs Ltd and took away a fur coat. Edith Waugh was later able to identify it as hers because of slight damage to one of the sleeves caused, she said, by a passing car throwing up some tar when she was out motoring.

Mrs Chandler was at this time staying with relatives in Buck-haven, in Scotland, and on April 15 she was called upon by Inspector James McCallum of the Fife Constabulary, told that police had recovered Mrs Waugh's stolen fur coat from Ralli's and could she explain why it turned out to be the coat she had sold to that company in December.

Mrs Chandler had an instant explanation, but curiously a different one to that which she had given earlier to Gertrude Murfitt, that she had bought it off a friend in Scotland. She acquired the coat, she told the inspector, when she went to Newmarket races with Bill Murfitt in the October and won £70 on the horses. As she was waiting for Mr Murfitt to come away from the stand she fell into conversation with a woman and her daughter sitting in a Daimler next to his Buick. The woman, hearing of Mrs Chandler's success, bemoaned her own rotten luck and said she had lost a lot of money. Then, Mrs Chandler told the inspector, the woman made the surprising suggestion that she would sell her the fur coat she was wearing to make up for her losses that day. When she saw the woman was serious about the offer, Mrs Chandler said she asked how much she wanted for it and was told that although the mink had cost more than £120 the woman would accept £80. Mrs Chandler demurred and the woman then said she would take £60, to which Mrs Chandler agreed and paid her the money out of her winnings. There was no question of a receipt, Mrs Chandler said, because she paid cash.

She told the inspector that she put the coat in the back of Murfitt's Buick, which was unlocked, and covered it with a rug. When Murfitt returned to the car they drove to the Subscription Rooms, one of his clubs, in the centre of Newmarket, where they were met by Murfitt's chauffeur, Ted Kydd, who had driven from Risby in the Ford Eight. Ted Kydd got into the Buick to drive Mrs Chandler home and left the smaller car for Murfitt to drive himself home later. When she got back to Hall Farm, she said she took the coat out of the car and took it indoors, where she showed it to Walker and told him she had bought it.

'I still remember what he said, he told me I was a damned fool because the coat may have been stolen, and that I should have obtained a receipt. I must admit, it never occurred to me that I should have done.' she told Inspector McCallum.

To the inspector, who knew little of the background to the coat, or in fact to Mrs Chandler, the story sounded plausible enough. He said he would pass on the information to the Newmarket police.

The same day that Inspector MacCallum interviewed Mrs Chandler, James Walker set off from Hall Farm in Billy Murfitt's car for Scotland – his own had been damaged in a crash – transferred to a train at Peterborough and reached Buckhaven the next day. Whether it was coincidence, or whether he received a telephone call from Mrs Chandler, no-one knew. Mrs Chandler told him of the interrogation by Inspector McCallum, whom he met two days later.

Walker and Mrs Chandler returned to Risby on April 19, but by then the Newmarket police were widening their investigation, interviewing Ted Kydd and Murfitt about what happened at the racecourse and Mrs Murfitt about what Mrs Chandler had told her when she first showed her the mink coat. It soon became apparent that Mrs Chandler's version of events differed from those of Murfitt, his wife and the chauffeur. The case against Mrs Chandler was set down for hearing by magistrates at Newmarket Petty Sessions on June 16.

**Riddle of the
white lilies**

Seventeen
Riddle of the white lilies

THE DROUGHT THAT HAD BESET East Anglia at the beginning of May had given way in June to gales and torrential storms. Roads were flooded, fields were awash and in the water meadows beside the River Lark around Bury St Edmunds, cattle were marooned. There was almost continuous rain during the Suffolk Show, held this year on the edge of Bury, and in one fearsome storm stands were damaged and marquees blown away. The weather replaced Bill Murfitt's death as the prime topic of conversation.

The national press, fickle in its search for interest, had withdrawn all but a few of its reporters as the painstaking but undramatic investigation went on in and around Risby. Some news reporters were diverted a few miles north to the Norfolk border where magistrates were hearing the case against Rose Emma Sandford who was accused of murdering her husband.

Mr Sandford had died suddenly at his home in the town of Dereham and, after information was given to the police about Rose Sandford's association with a lover, her husband's body was exhumed and his organs analysed by the ubiquitous analyst Roche Lynch, who discovered traces of strychnine. The Scotland Yard detectives called to investigate this case thought they had enough evidence to convict the pregnant, 27-years-old wife but after a three-day hearing at Downham Market the magistrates said they could find no prima facie case against her which would justify her being sent for trial to the Assizes. As a result, she was set free to tell the News of the World of her ordeal at the hands of British justice, for which she was being handsomely paid.

Burt wondered if there was any connection between the Norfolk case and Murfitt's death, even if it had only been to give his poisoner the macabre idea. Mrs Sandford had been arrested only six days before Murfitt died and the papers would have been full of it. But whatever the reason, Burt was pleased it had taken some of the spotlight off his work at Risby.

• •

When the detectives had arrived back from London after a weekend off they found a file of newspaper cuttings on Burt's desk telling how a bunch of white lilies had been left on Murfitt's grave to which were attached a card with the words, 'To know all is to understand all'. It was unsigned. Stories in some of the national newspapers told how a woman telephoned Risby post office and asked the postmistress, Connie Theobold, if she knew where exactly in the graveyard Murfitt's grave was. Mrs Theobold told her, at the gate by the back of the church. She asked the woman her name but she declined to give it, saying that she had motored over and wanted to show her respects with flowers. 'She sounded very agitated,' Connie told the reporters, while the photographer went off to St Giles church-yard to photograph the mysterious bouquet and its card. Frank Williams, The East Anglian Daily Times reporter in Bury St Edmunds, was sceptical about the whole matter, writing in his paper that the discovery of the flowers 'introduced an element of sensation into the inquiries,' adding, 'What is the meaning of this enigmatical wording, hurriedly produced in pencil on a card? The possibility that it may be due to an unfortunate hoax cannot be ruled out. Such an incident only adds to the work of the police.'

The story behind the white lilies came out later. Fed up with the lack of new angles on the Murfitt investigation the reporters still in the area decided to invent one for themselves. It was the Daily Mirror photographer who organised the flowers and he got one of the secretaries on his news desk in London to make the telephone call to the village Post Office.

The West Suffolk Chief Constable was furious and talked of the irresponsibility of the Press. Burt and Spooner shrugged it off. They had seen these tricks before and thought them harmless.

• •

Press coverage of the police investigations had given Bury what the Bury Free Press described as 'national notoriety,' which also became international when two American news agencies sent reporters from their London offices to ensure that newspaper readers in the United States were kept up-to-date with the unfolding scandal in a quiet Suffolk village. With a month now passed since Murfitt had died, Risby had become something of a tourist attraction, the newspapers reporting that parties of motor cars were driving to the village from far afield, especially at weekends. They drove slowly past Quays Farm, some of the cars parking on the roadside while their curious occupants got out and just stared at the farm-house, some taking photographs with their Box Brownies.

PC Carrington cycled up from Hengrave one Sunday afternoon to control the traffic after Reginald Burrell got one of his maids to telephone with a complaint that there was a traffic jam which had held up his chauffeur while driving some of his weekend guests to Bury station. Frank Orbell at the village shop found his weekend takings considerably increased as families stopped to buy sweets and lemonade and tried to engage him and his wife in conversation about the murder. Cars also lined the road outside the Crown and Castle while visitors went inside with the intention of buying drinks for any villager who might pass a tit-bit of information, which some of them did without necessarily being in a position to prove what they said was accurate.

• •

Reg Spooner always made a point of writing regularly to his wife Myra whenever cases took him away from home. He had done so even before their marriage in 1929, and although when he was in London he didn't get home until late most nights, he still missed the warmth and companionship of his home life and needed to keep in touch. He complained in one letter that he and Burt had now become celebrities in Bury St Edmunds, and that was making their work more difficult. Wherever they went, he wrote, they were recognised – shopkeepers, newsboys, ordinary people in the street liked to say hello. 'I should think that it's practically impossible here for anybody to do anything at all without everybody else knowing about it – a real hotbed of scandal and gossip,' he wrote.

Some of the gossip Spooner had come across was of the sort he had heard from the customers in the Crown and Castle – loose, frivolous talk most of it, but which needed to be checked out. He had gone to see the gamekeeper, Moki Spalding, who had a row with Murfitt over shooting rights, the shepherd Bill Thomson, who had been sacked, and Jim Bennett whom Murfitt had banned from parking on his land, and he was certain there was no possibility of any of them being suspects.

Burt had been told that the foreman, Syd Williams, could have had a grudge against his boss because Murfitt had offered a job as farm manager to his niece's husband, Jimmy Smythe, and Williams feared his job was in danger. Burt found, to the contrary, that Williams had welcomed the appointment because it would lighten his already heavy workload and Smythe would also be taking over some of the work done by the farm secretary, Mollie Targett, who was leaving shortly to get married.

Burt was also told by Mrs Murfitt of suggestions made to her by Elaine Browne that Bill Murfitt was over-fond of Ricky, his daughter-in-law, and Valerie Smythe, his niece, and in the search for any possible motive the detectives had to follow up every lead. Mrs Murfitt said she thought Mrs Browne only made the suggestions because she was jealous and Burt was convinced, certainly in the case of Ricky Murfitt, that there was no truth in the rumour.

As to Valerie Smythe, Mrs Murfitt did admit that her husband had bought several items of riding wear for his niece, but she thought this was just because Valerie did not have a father. Burt, in his searches through Quays Farm, did come across a letter to Murfitt written in endearing terms to 'My very dearest Bill,' when Valerie and Jimmy were running a coffee plantation in India. Much of the letter was about the mundane social life of the British colony there – race meetings, tennis matches and dances – but there were also hints of a very close relationship between uncle and niece. At one point Valerie had written, 'I'm not really bad, just naughty. I always seem to have more men friends than women.' She also wrote, 'It's marvellous to know that you are so fond of me and willing to do and give me so much. I will not be too jealous of Mrs B, we must all have our friends and flutters... take care of your dear self and I hope to be coming home and going to a dance with you, and I shall hope to make Mrs B just a little jealous.' It was signed, 'Yours very lovingly, Val.' Burt knew that Mrs B was Mrs Murfitt, or Mrs Bill as she was known to some family and friends. But on reading the letter a second time he decided that, even if there was a stronger than normal relationship between Murfitt and his niece, given what Valerie had to gain by his staying alive he could not see how she could have a motive for seeing him dead.

Eighteen **The fur coat case opens**

Eighteen
The fur coat case opens

In mid-June there began a series of four legal hearings in West Suffolk which ensured that Murfitt's murder and the case that was now linked with it – the allegations of theft of a fur coat against Mrs Chandler – was back on the newspapers' front pages for a five-week period. The petty sessions hearing against Mrs Chandler was to be followed on June 24 by the opening of the full inquest into Murfitt's death. On July 5 was to come the resumption of the case against Mrs Chandler at quarter sessions with the final day of the inquest being held on July 21. The mixed timings of the hearings caused some confusion to those who did not know the full background to the cases. They were also a legal minefield for lawyers, magistrates and the coroner alike, all of whom had to take care that evidence given at one hearing did not prejudice evidence given at another.

The scene outside Newmarket Petty Sessions courthouse on Thursday June 16 had something of the atmosphere of Ladies Day at Ascot. Women in flowered summer dresses and fashionable hats waited outside the main doors. The case had caught the imagination of the racing town and those who secured a seat in the public gallery would be able to give first-hand accounts of the proceedings to friends at cocktail parties and dinners afterwards.

As Leonard Burt and Reg Spooner drove into the police station car park next to the courthouse they recognised several Fleet Street reporters and photographers in the crowd. The detectives knew they themselves would get very little out of the day's hearing, during which Newmarket magistrates would decide if the police had enough evidence to prove a prima facie case against Mrs Chandler and, if so, to enable them to send her to West Suffolk Quarter Sessions for a full hearing. This first hearing would just produce evidence by prosecution witnesses, which the detectives had both read in full beforehand anyway, and any cross examination of them which Mrs Chandler's counsel cared to make. She would not be required to give evidence until the quarter sessions.

The Scotland Yard detectives joined local policeman and court officials as they walked through the entrance from the police station into the courtroom, where legal teams for prosecution and defence were already waiting. As soon as the court doors were opened the reporters rushed in, vying for the seats nearest the bench. The public seats were filled seconds later and the court ushers had to hold back those who could not get a seat and move them back out into the street.

William Murfitt, extreme right, on his horse at a
meeting of the hunt

At ten o'clock the door in the panelling behind the bench opened and an usher called for all to stand as the four magistrates took their seats. When her name was called Mrs Chandler walked from the back of the court to the dock, near which James Walker was sitting with a notebook already opened and a pencil in his hand. She was wearing a dark blue costume with a black, wide-brimmed hat and she smiled briefly and nervously at Walker as she passed. A buzz of conversation arose and the clerk had to call for quiet.

The two summonses against Mrs Chandler were read out, one of receiving a mink fur coat knowing it to have been stolen and the other of stealing the coat, and the defence counsel, Mr B K Featherstone, told the court his client strenuously denied the allegations.

The prosecution case was outlined by Thomas Ashton, member of a family firm of solicitors in Bury St Edmunds. His brother John had been involved in the early preparation of the case but, as he discovered that he had played badminton with Mrs Chandler and others at Bury Corn Exchange from time to time, he had withdrawn from the case.

Mr Ashton summarised the evidence that was to be given – how Mrs Edith Waugh had noticed the coat missing from her wardrobe on September 29, 1937, after seeing it there the day before, how she did not see the coat again until April after police had recovered it from a London furriers, and she confirmed it was hers. The furriers told police they had bought the coat from Mrs Chandler who, when she was interviewed, claimed she had bought it from a woman at Newmarket racecourse, which she had attended with Mr Murfitt. Mr Ashton also told how Murfitt had driven Mrs Chandler to his club, and how his chauffeur had driven Mrs Chandler home from there.

The first witness, Charles Wolff, a furrier in business at Argyll Street, London, confirmed that he sold a mink coat to Mrs Waugh in October 1935. He nodded his head when asked to identify her in court. To the best of his belief the coat produced in court was that which he sold her. Yes, he told defence counsel who rose to cross examine him, the coat was made in his factory, adding cautiously, 'All I can say is that I sold a coat of similar style to Mrs Waugh.'

Mrs Waugh was next in the witness box, immaculate in a pearl grey costume and constantly fingering a lorgnette as she repeated how she missed her coat from the wardrobe and how, when it was found, she identified it by the slight damage to the sleeve. Mr Featherstone asked her about her three domestic staff, hoping to imply that one of them could be responsible for the theft. Only one still had her job, Mrs Waugh said somewhat crossly. The other two, one Swiss and the other Spanish, who had access to her bedroom, had been dismissed.

Asked when Walker and Mrs Chandler last visited her house she remembered it was about January 17, 1937, when they came to collect a photograph of her daughter's wedding. She was not there but they spoke to her daughter Peggy. When did she first hear the coat had been found? On April 20, 1938, when Walker telephoned and told her it had been purchased on the racecourse from some unknown woman. Spooner did a quick check on Mrs Waugh's statement and the fact that Walker had broken the news to Mrs Waugh about the coat's discovery was not in it.

Inspector Dudley Butcher gave evidence that he inspected Mrs Waugh's bedroom soon after the coat was found to be missing and although valuable jewellery and other furs were in the room they were left untouched. There was no sign of forcible entry. He interviewed the servants and was not able to produce any witness who saw Mrs Chandler in the house on September 28th or 29th, or even at any time during 1937. Burt frowned because that last statement had the effect of weakening Mrs Waugh's evidence, not importantly but it was a nuisance.

The inspector said he interviewed Walker, who backed up Mrs Chandler's version of events. Mr Featherstone asked, 'And he gave you all the information you required?'

Inspector Butcher was non-committal. 'He made a statement.'

This time Burt smiled. Knowing Walker, he could realise the difficulty the inspector had in getting information out of the farmer.

The inspector stepped down and there was another buzz of anticipation in the court as the name of Gertrude Murfitt was called. She entered the room with her son Leslie and his wife Ricky following behind and Leslie escorted her to the dock. Her frailty and her pallid complexion were emphasised by her black costume trimmed with white and a large black hat with a veil covering her face. She told the court how Mrs Chandler had shown her the coat and said she wanted to sell it on behalf of a friend and how she eventually went with her to London to help her sell it. In answer to Mr Featherstone she said yes, she and Mrs Chandler had been great friends at the time and no, Mrs Chandler never at any time mentioned that she had bought the coat at Newmarket races. Her evidence over, Mrs Murfitt was escorted to the back of the court by her son.

Next in the witness box was Inspector James McCallum, who told how he interviewed Mrs Chandler in Scotland, when she told him she had bought the coat at the races and later sold it in London. By this time, with the constant repetition of the main facts, most of the reporters had stopped taking notes and were staring ahead vacantly. Their boredom was then relieved by a touch of farce as the wary Scottish policeman became involved in an argument with Mr Featherstone, who asked if he could examine the officer's notebook, a request the inspector declined.

The barrister asked, sarcastically, if it was the practice in Scotland to refuse to produce notebooks.

Inspector McCallum waved his notebook at the barrister and said, 'The notebook is produced,' without offering to hand it over.

The magistrates agreed with Mr Featherstone that he should be allowed to inspect the notebook and the inspector walked across and showed him the pages relating to the case. The inspector refused to let the solicitor take the notebook in his hand, saying truculently, 'He wants to delve into my notebook. I don't know why, but he's not going to.'

Thomas Ashton looked embarrassed and asked the inspector to hand the notebook to the clerk of the court, who said that the only other entries in the book related to a completely different case.

The last witness was Murfitt's chauffeur, Ted Kydd, who said he waited in the Ford Eight at Newmarket Subscription Rooms for Murfitt, who arrived in the Buick with Mrs Chandler in the front seat beside him. Kydd said he took Murfitt's place at the wheel of the Buick and drove Mrs Chandler to Hall Farm. She did not take anything out of the car. She was wearing a fur coat, which was not the one produced for him to examine in court. She was carrying only a card, which he thought was a race card.

Mr Featherstone cross examined him. How long did he take to drive from Newmarket to Risby? About ten minutes, the chauffeur said. How far is it? About ten miles. Yes, he agreed, he often drove at over sixty miles an hour, adding with a sidelong glance at the police presence in court, 'except in the built-up areas.'

With the prosecution evidence completed, Mr Featherstone rose to submit that on the charge alleging theft there was no evidence to show Mrs Chandler was at the Waugh's house at any material time. On the charge of receiving, there was no evidence that his client knew that the coat had been stolen, and her subsequent conduct could only be described as that of a person who was absolutely innocent. No jury would convict on the evidence produced, he said. The housekeeper nodded in agreement and Walker made a note in his book.

The Bench retired briefly and when the magistrates returned their chairman said they had decided no prima facie case had been made on the theft charge, but that on the receiving charge Mrs Chandler would be committed for trial at the West Suffolk Quarter Sessions on July 5th.

The chairman said Mrs Chandler would be allowed bail on putting up her own surety of £50, with another surety required of £100. Burt saw Walker catch the eye of Mr Featherstone and raise his pencil to indicate he would stand surety. He then walked close beside Mrs Chandler out of the court and when she ran towards his car which was parked a few yards away he held up his mackintosh to protect her from the stare of the waiting crowd, and from the flash of the cameras as the photographers surged towards her.

Burt knew the police did not have much of a case on the theft charge and was not surprised when the magistrates threw it out. When it came to the charge of receiving the coat, it would depend how much she could lie. It was also no surprise when Walker had put up the bail surety, because it was obvious that he was besotted with her. But after reading the report on her background, Burt thought there might also be an undercurrent of fear from him about what his housekeeper might do next, particularly in view of what she had done to the farmer's car in a fit of rage.

Nineteen Walker's car is sabotaged

Nineteen

Walker's car is sabotaged

JAMES WALKER'S MOTHER WAS A WIDOW, in her 80s and wealthy. As she lived in a hotel in Matlock, Derbyshire, she welcomed the invitations from her son to visit him for two or three months a year and enjoy his garden and the Suffolk countryside. Every two or three years Mrs Walker would take her son out and buy him a new car. She was always surprised that his house-keeper, Mrs Chandler, went with them and seemed to be the one that made the choice but she held her tongue because she didn't want to upset her son.

Increasingly, Mrs Chandler came to resent Mrs Walker's visits and when she came to stay with them in 1935 the housekeeper went off in a huff to live with friends for a while. When she returned she found Walker's new Triumph sports car in the garage, and because she had not been involved in its purchase she was furious. She said she hated the car – she told Gertrude Murfitt so, and Mr and Mrs Berry.

Mrs Walker was due to return to Derbyshire in a few days time and as a last treat Walker drove her in his new car to Felixstowe for a day out by the sea. Mrs Chandler refused to go and stayed in bed most of the day. On the seafront the Berrys met Walker and his mother and the latter was in an upset and nervous state. Mrs Walker told the Berrys that when her son went to get the car out of the garage that morning he found Mrs Chandler there going berserk and attacking the tyres with a pair of scissors.

That was not all. As they were driving to Felixstowe they heard funny noises coming from the engine and when they pulled into a garage at Stowmarket for an engineer to look at it he found someone had been interfering with the mechanism. It could have been dangerous if it had not been seen to. Then, as they arrived in Felixstowe, Walker said the wheels were feeling wobbly and when he parked he found some of the nuts had been loosened.

A few days later, when Mr Berry telephoned Walker to invite him and Fernie over for a game of cards, the farmer told him he no longer had the car. It had been destroyed in a fire while it was parked in the garage. The flames had spread from the car and destroyed not only the garage but also a granary to which it was attached, both of which were owned by his landlord, Hengrave Estates.

Mr Berry told Burt about the car fire soon after his arrival in Bury and the detective looked up the local police report on the incident. He found that Walker had been driving home at about 11pm when he was stopped by a Constable and told that his offside light was not working. He didn't think much about it and when he got home he parked the car in the garage and went to bed. At about 2.45am he was woken up by the barking of dogs and when he looked out he saw flames leaping up from the garage and granary. There was a big flash as a can of petrol kept in garage exploded.

Because the car was so badly damaged the insurers could not say what had caused the fire, but after hearing Walker's story of the failed light they put it down, not without doubts, to an electrical defect and paid Walker £200 insurance for the car, plus another £120 to Walker's landlord. What the insurance men didn't know was that when Walker went to bed that night Mrs Chandler had said she would not be retiring until later because she had to lay a fire in one of the grates for lighting next day. The farmer was a little surprised at this, because it was a task she had previously left to the servants. The police now thought she was right about laying the fire – but she had done it in the garage.

The police report on Mrs Chandler said her mother put her strange behaviour down to a bad fall when she was a child, when she banged her head and it wouldn't stop bleeding. Burt thought he knew a lot of people who had bad knocks when they were younger, but that did not make them unscrupulous liars, thieves or arsonists when they grew up.

• •

The publicity in the newspapers about Mrs Chandler's appearance in court, and the increasing rumours about her possible involvement in Murfitt's death, raised more suspicions about the activities of Walker's housekeeper. Edith Waugh, for example, began to think back to the death of her sister, Walker's wife Minnie, who had died so suddenly in 1926 at the age of 48. Up to the time of her death Minnie had been in good health and took a keen interest in the farm, but on the night of June 8 she told Walker she felt unwell and went to bed. The next morning she was dead.

When he was given the information Burt checked back on Minnie Walker's death certificate. He found the cause of death was given as cerebral haemorrhage and Raynaud's disease. Information for the certificate was given by Walker, who was present at the death. The GP who signed it, Dr Gough Kilner, had now died and no post mortem had been held.

Some of Minnie Walker's family now began to wonder if she was poisoned by either Walker or Chandler, or both, so that Mrs Chandler could come and live with him at Risby. Walker had been difficult to pin down when he met Mrs Chandler. On one occasion he said he knew her in 1924, which would have been after she arrived in London from India. Following that she went to live for a while in Scotland, and Walker had lived there before moving to Suffolk, so they could have met up there. Also, her husband in India was a chemist, and she could well have got a knowledge of poisons from him. Burt knew they had to look at all the possibilities.

Spooner went to Newmarket to speak to Mrs Waugh, and to the neighbouring village of Fordham to speak to Minnie Walker's family. Mrs Waugh's daughter Peggy said she was convinced that Walker and Mrs Chandler, whom she referred to as 'The Snake', had poisoned her Aunt Minnie and was all for having her body dug up from Risby churchyard, but Mrs Waugh was against the idea. Burt made his own investigations in Risby and could find no evidence that Mrs Chandler had been seen in the village until she arrived as housekeeper in the December of 1926 and the detectives decided to drop that part of the investigation.

• •

By the beginning of July the investigation into the murder of William Murfitt had been going on just over six weeks and Burt's frustration at not having enough evidence to make a criminal charge was beginning to show. He had not completely discounted the possibility that Mrs Murfitt had poisoned her husband, or that Mr or Mrs Browne could be responsible, but his suspicions were now definitely centred on Mrs Chandler, and less so on Walker. He had become fed up with the couple's constant change of story and their obvious lies, but he knew he had no proof that either of them had got into Quays Farm to place the cyanide in the salts.

Burt had been warned by the West Suffolk Chief Constable, Colin Robertson, that the Bury Coroner, Thomas Wilson, had been asking how the investigations into Murfitt's death were proceeding. If there was any chance of a charge being preferred against anyone he would happily postpone the inquest, but if no real progress had been made he said he intended going ahead during July.

The problem for Burt with an inquest was that the Coroner could only conduct the hearing to establish the cause and the reason for death – accident, misadventure, manslaughter or murder. He did not hold a trial, he conducted an inquiry. As the law stood, it was possible for an inquest jury to return a verdict of murder by a named person and that person could be sent direct to Assizes without appearing first in a magistrates court on a committal hearing, but that was a rarity. But Burt knew they would be lucky for that to happen on the evidence they had to date and he did not hope for much more when he heard the Coroner had set the date for the resumed inquest for June 24th.

Twenty **Mrs Murfitt's inquest ordeal**

Twenty

Mrs Murfitt's inquest ordeal

THOMAS WILSON DIDN'T LIKE MUCH of what he knew so far about the Murfitt case. A man with an intense local pride, he thought the revelations of scandal and intrigue which he had read in the witnesses' depositions did nothing for the county he had been born to serve, like his family before him. As Coroner for the Liberty of Bury St Edmunds he held a position which used to be filled by the local lord of the manor's family and which had been in his family since the Middle Ages. Coroners, he would say, are born, not made. In Bury St Edmunds, the Coroner's position was in the gift of his cousin, who had appointed him to the job, and he was comfortable with the fact that his wife's brother was Deputy Coroner and he hoped the line would go on for years.

When the Great War came Thomas Wilson had joined up immediately and the correct touch of authority and arrogance which had come with his Haileybury education, followed by some ten years in the family firm of solicitors, had ensured him an automatic commission. He went to Gibraltar Barracks in Bury St Edmunds and enlisted in the sixth Cyclist Battalion of the Suffolk Regiment, later transferring to the Queen's Westminster Rifles. By the time he left the army with the rank of Major in the winter of 1919 he had endured hard and often inhuman experience in France, Ireland and the Middle East and was the proud holder of the Military Cross. He liked to tell the story of how he was handed his medal by the King while he was in his pyjamas – although Wilson had not been wounded there was a shortage of patients when His Majesty visited a hospital for the presentation and he was sent away to change out of his uniform to make it look better for the photographers. He was also lucky. After one battle against the Turks he and his batman were lost in the desert when they came across a lone Australian, who gave them bearings which he said would get them to safety. The two set off, only to find their horses were reluctant to proceed in the direction they had been given, and when the Britons decided to give the horses their head they immediately turned round and headed in the opposite direction towards their own lines. The Aussie's faulty navigation had been directing them straight towards the Turks.

Now in his mid-50s, Thomas Wilson held several other public positions in addition to that of Coroner, being Under-Sheriff of the county, clerk to two benches of magistrates and Town Clerk of Bury St Edmunds, while in his spare time he was secretary of the Suffolk Hunt, with which he rode enthusiastically. He was the sort of man without whom a town could not function efficiently, and he meant to make sure it didn't have the chance to do so without him for a very long time.

The inquest into the death of William Murfitt, which had been opened briefly and then adjourned the day after he died, was resumed on Friday, June 24, at Risby Village Hall. Thomas Wilson had already had a preliminary meeting with the Chief Constable and Chief Inspector Burt, he knew the line their investigations were taking and he had told them openly he did not know how much he could help them. This inquest was particularly difficult, he said, because one of the witnesses was involved in unfinished legal proceedings – he was referring to Mrs Chandler and the fur coat case – and he would have to take a fine line to ensure that her position at her forthcoming trial was not prejudiced, whatever the possibility that she might be involved in the farmer's death.

When Wilson arrived at the village hall just after 9.30am there was already a large crowd outside the main entrance and members of the jury were starting to arrive, one or two in cars and the others on bicycles. Witnesses, including the Murfitt family and the Brownes, stood at the back of the hall with farm employees and other villagers waiting to be shown where they were to sit, while Fernie Chandler stood outside uncomplainingly as the photographers took their pictures. Burt, Spooner and Superintendent Brinkley were already in their seats near the front, exchanging papers and conferring. Dr Roche Lynch, eminent Home Office Analyst, was seated to one side, peeping out from behind the piano which was covered decorously for the day by a green cloth. When all the chairs reserved for the public were filled Pc Carrington ushered those unlucky enough not to get seats back through the main door to the accompaniment of muttered complaints.

Thomas Wilson opened the hearing sharp on 10am. The same two protagonists from the fur coat case at Newmarket stood and announced their presence: Thomas Ashton, the local solicitor representing Mrs Murfitt and her family, and Mr Featherstone, the barrister from London, who said that he had been instructed to watch the proceedings on behalf of 'certain interested parties'.

He gave the inquest an immediate air of mystery by proclaiming that it might become necessary for him to ask permission to question a certain witness or witnesses, and if he did he would disclose to the Coroner the identity of the party or parties instructing him and he would leave it to the

Coroner to decide whether he revealed that information to the jury. 'However, I submit respectfully,' he said, 'that as this is a Coroner's court, where there is no accused person, it would be undesirable and not in the interests of justice for that information to be disclosed to the jury.'

The jury and members of the public looked bemused while anyone with inside knowledge knew he was looking after the interests of Mrs Chandler and Walker. Wilson, without comment, quickly passed on with his own address to the jury.

It was for them to decide how William Murfitt met his death, he said, and he thought their conclusion would be that he died from poisoning. If that was so, it was for them to say whether that poison was taken by mistake or accident. Alternatively, they might think he took the poison intending to take his own life, in which case their verdict would be suicide. 'Or you might think,' he said, with the room now completely silent, 'that some other person disposed the poison in such a way that Mr Murfitt took it unwittingly. If you think that, then that person would be guilty of murder.'

The Coroner then asked all 31 witnesses who had been subpoenaed to attend to come forward and told them of their rights. They could not refuse to be sworn, he said, but they could refuse to answer any question. They should put out of their minds anything they might have read in the Press about the case – 'which has enjoyed a large degree of publicity' he added with a hint of distaste in his voice.

After the initial heavy atmosphere of mystery and warnings the undramatic evidence of the first witnesses came as something of a relief. Murfitt's horse-keeper Charles Palmer told how he saw his boss in the farmyard at about 6 o'clock on the morning of May 17, and there was nothing unusual about that. The gardener, George Howard, said Murfitt had given him a bottle of cyanide to get rid of wasps nests, which he did before burying the bottle as he always did. This interested the jury, one of whom wanted to know when he last used cyanide. Just before the fruit was gathered, George said. Which fruit was that, asked the Coroner. Plums said George, and Burt began to wonder, at this rate, how many days the inquest would last if they had to cover all the various and bountiful harvests which the village produced in order to establish relevant dates.

Jack Gibbons, the village postman, said Murfitt took the post from him when he called at 6.45am, something which he often did. Syd Williams the foreman, said he saw Murfitt just before seven and did not notice anything unusual about him. The reporters, some of which had left London early that morning to get to Risby in time for the inquest, began to yawn. The first reference to death came when Williams related how, later, he was called to the house, told his boss was ill, and then learned that he had died.

The Coroner asked Williams if he knew that Jimmy Smythe, who had been a farm pupil under him, was coming to work at the farm and whether it would affected his position. Smythe's coming would not have done him any harm, he replied, yes he had been on good terms with Murfitt and no, he didn't know anyone who had a grudge against his boss. There was just a hint of suspicion and motive and the reporters jotted it all down.

The first real sign of interest from the Press bench and from the public seats came when Gertrude Murfitt was called. Wearing a black dress with a large white collar, and with a grey hat trimmed with black, the nervous, slightly trembling widow walked from the back of the hall and the Coroner allowed her to sit at a table in front of him. He began by taking her through the part of her statement describing how her husband had taken the Fynnon salts and almost immediately afterwards collapsed on the floor. In what some thought was a macabre gesture, Dr Roche Lynch stepped forward from behind the piano and produced the very tin of salts which had contained the poison dose and placed it on the table in front of Mrs Murfitt. She glanced away before carrying on with her evidence. She had just got to the point where Dr Ware arrived at Quays Farm in answer to the telephone call from Mollie Targett when the Coroner adjourned the hearing for lunch.

As the court rose Reg Spooner, who had gone outside for a cigarette during some of the more mundane evidence, appeared at the main door and caught Burt's attention. When the inspector got to the door Spooner pointed out an agitated James Walker who was pacing up and down under the elm trees which framed the road leading to Quays Farm. At one point he went and sat on the step of a stile with his hands over his face before getting up and walking up and down again.

After the lunch-break at the farmhouse Gertrude Murfitt allowed her son Leslie to drive her back the 200 yards to the village hall and she walked in beside him, looking straight ahead and showing recognition of no-one. There were more questions for her from the Coroner about what happened on the fatal morning, after which he turned to whether she had bought any cyanide at any time. This time she tried to clear up the mistake she had made in her statement to Burt. 'I don't remember buying any cyanide but I am told I did, and it may be that I did as I bought most things of that kind for the farm,' she said, and the Coroner did not pursue the matter.

She was asked about her trip to see her sister the day before Murfitt's death and whether any outsider had been in Quays Farm that day. Yes, she remembered, the rector, just before she set out for Wisbech. Wilson obviously did not think him a suspect and passed on to who else visited the house frequently. Mr and Mrs Browne, she said, Mr Walker and Mrs Chandler, and a few friends who lived further away. 'Were Mr Walker, Mrs Chandler and Mrs and Mrs Browne intimate with you?' asked the Coroner. 'Quite so,' replied Mrs Murfitt. The Coroner used 'intimate' in the context of a close friendship, but his wording caused a few sly smiles round the room. He then turned to the friendship with the Brownes and was more precise.

'Had there been certain trouble between you and your husband over Mrs Browne?' – 'Yes, there was a little bit of trouble over Mrs Browne.' She was trying to play it down, but her shame and embarrassment was now total. The Coroner, reading from her statement, had to drag it out of her sentence by sentence.

'You say it was got over. What was that trouble and when was it got over?' – 'About 18 months or two years ago.'

'How was it got over? Was it got over by your husband ceasing to have anything to do with Mrs Browne?' – 'Yes.'

'She kept on coming to the house?' – 'Yes.'

The Coroner insisted on her saying what the trouble was. 'Was it on the ground that your husband had been committing acts of intimacy with Mrs Brown?' – 'Yes.' Gertrude was now blushing heavily and her voice was almost inaudible.

'And had you reason to think that these acts had ceased?' – 'Yes.'

Did Mrs Browne continue to be your friend? – 'Yes.'

'Did Mr Browne know about this? – 'I understand not. I do not think he knew.'

To Gertrude's relief, the Coroner then went on to talk about her friendship with Walker and Mrs Chandler. When the Brownes stopped coming so frequently they visited quite a lot, she said. That was about a year ago. They both knew the dining room well. She didn't think either of them had seen her or her husband taking salts, but the tin was always on the sideboard and anyone who came could see it.

Mrs Murfitt told how Mrs Chandler came straight up to her bedroom at Quays Farm one day and knocked on the door.

'Did that intimate friendship continue until the time of your husband's death?' 'No.'

'When did it cease?' – 'There were rumours about Mrs Chandler, so my husband said I was not to have anything further to do with her.'

The Coroner then took her through the part of her statement referring to her knowledge of the fur coat case, and she agreed she knew Mrs Chandler had gone to the Newmarket races with Murfitt. Mrs Murfitt said she saw Walker after she had made a statement to the police and told him she was very sorry she had been brought into the case, but she had just told the police the truth.

On the morning her husband died, she said, Walker went to her house to sympathise with her. When he left he said, 'Remember, Gertrude, we never let our friends down.' She thought he was angry with her about the fact that she was to give evidence about the fur coat.

The Coroner asked if she had ever heard her husband suggest he was going to commit suicide – 'No, never,' she replied. She had not noticed anything unusual about him before his death, in fact he had seemed in much better health lately, and they had not had any serious difference of opinion recently. They had no arguments about young Billy leaving home – they were sad about it but they thought it would do him good.

Then back to any other possible scandals. 'Did you know of any illicit relations between your husband and any woman recently?' 'No, I do not think there were any at all.'

'Was there any woman of whom you were jealous?' 'No, none whatever.'

One of the last questions to her was 'Was the tin of salts in its usual place on the sideboard on the morning of the Tuesday?' 'No, it was on the right had side instead of the left.' Interest stirred on the press table again.

After three hours of giving evidence, the worst three hours of her life Gertrude considered it, she got up from her chair and walked to sit at the back of the court.

There followed evidence by Dr Ware about how he was called to attend to Murfitt, and how he later removed some of the organs from his body. Dr Roche Lynch, in a thin, piercing voice, told how he examined the organs and the salts and how, after a variety of tests, deduced the poison must have been put in the salts in the early morning of May 17th.

When Mollie Targett was called to give her evidence the Coroner, showing signs of weariness as the warm afternoon wore on, became cross when he thought she was evading his questions. The loyal secretary said during the last two years the relationship between Mr and Mrs Murfitt had been very happy and she had never heard of matrimonial troubles.

Coroner: 'I have a statement here by you setting out all sorts of matrimonial troubles' – 'It is only what I have been told.'

Coroner: 'By Mrs Murfitt? You must be open with us or else we must treat you differently.'

Miss Targett, looking suitably chastised, agreed Mrs Murfitt had mentioned a woman named Kay, who was now married. Yes, she said, she had heard about the trouble over Mrs Browne but that was not existing at the time of Murfitt's death. She thought Mrs Murfitt was very fond of her husband and recently had not seen signs of anything but affection for him.

The repetition of what had happened at the time of Murfitt's death, who had bought cyanide and where, and what side of the sideboard the salts were found on, was beginning to wear down the alertness of everyone in the room. It was not until Doris Howard was called, well past everyone's normal tea time, that the day's hearing ended on a dramatic note. The parlour maid told how Mr Murfitt sent her out on an errand on the night of May 12 and when she returned she saw a woman walking near the churchyard, not far from Quays Farm.

'Did you recognise her?' asked the Coroner.

'It looked like Mrs Chandler,' Doris said.

The reporters took up their pencils again and the Coroner announced that the inquest would be adjourned until the next day.

While the afternoon session had been going on Spooner had seen Walker, still looking nervous and distressed, walking up and down the road outside the village hall. The farmer did not look as though he would get much sleep that night.

Twenty One **Mrs Chandler gives evidence**

Twenty One
Mrs Chandler gives evidence

EVERY SEAT IN RISBY VILLAGE HALL was again taken up on the Saturday morning when all present rose for the entry of Coroner Thomas Wilson at exactly 10.30am. Evidence given the day before about Bill Murfitt's infidelity had been the talk of the village's two pubs the previous night because, although stories about his relationship with Elaine Browne had been the subject of rumours before and after his death, this was the first time they had been publicly and officially aired. The reporters, able at last to record what many of them had already learned from their police contacts, had the satisfaction of seeing their reports given large spaces in that morning's newspapers. They were hoping for more spicy angles today, although the first witnesses only confirmed much of what had been given in evidence the day before.

The Coroner did question Beatrice Cutmore, the Murfitt's cook, closely about where she found the tin of salts when she dusted the sideboard on the morning her employer died.

'I want you to be careful about this,' the Coroner said, 'The position of this tin might be of considerable importance.'

Beatrice said she was certain it was on the right hand side of the tantalus, a position it had never been in before. Previously it had always been on the left.

Billy Murfitt, still tanned from his Mediterranean sea voyage, told how he had worked on the family's farms for about nine years, how there had been a short break when he found another job after a difference of opinion with his father but had returned to Risby until he went to sea in April that year.

The Coroner then quickly moved to more relevant matters. Did Billy know that his father and mother had a row about a lady? – Yes. Had they made up their difference? – Yes. Was it over Mrs Browne? – Yes. There was little new in it for the Press Bench.

The reporters perked up a little when Billy was asked about the keys to Quays Farm, one of which was still missing.

'Isn't it a fact that you broke into the house one night because you were out late and had no key?' the Coroner asked.

'Probably,' answered Billy defensively. 'Other people have done it before.'

There was a family row about it, he said, and he was given one of the new keys. He left it in his bedroom when he went away. No, he said, he had never left it in his car. Burt had wanted that question asked because he knew Walker had borrowed Billy's car at times and could have obtained a key that way.

Billy was followed by his elder brother Leslie, who gave evidence about the family and business finances, which were sound, and his wife Ricky related how she had gone to the farmhouse door to see Mrs Chandler when she called with the cake for Mrs Murfitt.

There was a buzz of greater interest when Rippon Charles Browne came forward to give evidence and was asked if he heard that Murfitt was on intimate terms with his wife.

'Not until... the Sunday after he died.'

'You tell the jury that prior to that you had no knowledge of it?' 'I had no knowledge until the Sunday after.'

Obviously embarrassed, and seeing the line of the Coroner's questioning, Mr Browne said he had never had a quarrel with Murfitt, he had never seen the tin of salts on the Murfitt's sideboard and he had not been in the Murfitt's house any time between the Sunday and the time when Murfitt died.

Browne showed further embarrassment when he was asked about his and his wife's sleeping habits. They slept in the same bed, he said, and his wife did not get up during the night before Murfitt died. The Coroner did not take the matter any further and adjourned for lunch.

As he left the main hall Coroner Thomas Wilson beckoned to Superintendent Brinkley and Chief Inspector Burt to follow him into the small room at the back. After a few minutes Brinkley came out, got into a police car and was driven off. When he came back just before the inquest resumed the Chief Constable, Captain Robertson, was with him and they walked together into the hall.

The afternoon's first witness, Richard Williams, whose wife was still recovering from the shock of having two Scotland Yard detectives in her house to look for poison, told the Coroner he had bought some cyanide the previous summer, half of which he put into a hornets nest and the rest he kept in his house in a bottle, which had been inspected by Sergeant

Spooner. He didn't sound a likely suspect and made way for the next witness, Inspector Dudley Butcher, whose main task was to confirm that had Murfitt still been alive he would have been called as a witness in the fur coat case, although he left the inquest guessing what that evidence would have been.

Then the Coroner's officer called James Walker. His thick-set figure exaggerated by a double-breasted grey suit, handkerchief in his top pocket, he sat in front of the Coroner looking calmer than he had when Spooner and Burt spotted him outside the hall. The first few questions were about how well he knew the Murfitts. Since 1937, he said, they visited each other's homes.

'Did you go to Quays Farm alone, or were you accompanied?' – 'Mrs Chandler was with me.'

'Who is Mrs Chandler? – 'She keeps house for me.' A few sly smiles in the public seats.

'How long have you known Mrs Chandler?' – 'I cannot say exactly, approximately 20 years.' Burt looked sideways at Spooner, who made a note in his book and circled it with his pencil. It was one of several different answers Walker had given to that question.

He said their friendly relationship with the Murfitts ended sometime before the farmer's death. At first he gave no explanation to the Coroner why this happened, but later said it was because while he was visiting Mrs Chandler in Scotland Inspector McCallum had asked him to advise her not to have anything to do with anyone involved in the fur coat case. Spooner made another note in his book. Walker had not mentioned that the friendship had ended because Murfitt accused Mrs Chandler of cheating at cards.

Wilson then asked, 'Can you say quite definitely and without any doubt that you were not in Mr Murfitt's house or on his premises around the house at any time between the morning of May 16 and the time of his death?' – 'I was not'

'So far as you know was Mrs Chandler on those premises at any time during that period? – 'No, definitely not.'

'How can you say that so definitely, because you did not even qualify it?' – 'Very well, as far as I know.' 'Were you with Mrs Chandler all the time I have stated?' – 'With very rare intervals.'

'Mrs Chandler and yourself occupied separate bedrooms?' Walker obviously misheard the question, or didn't want to answer it. 'No, I have my own room,' he replied.

Then there began a long exchange about Walker buying cyanide, during which he became confused and, by the look on their faces, so did several members of the jury.

Walker said he bought some on July 7th, 1937. It was in a white paper package.

The Coroner, 'Was it in a bottle or a package when you bought it?' – 'In a package.'

'And did you put it in a bottle?' No, I am sorry, the bottle was wrapped in white paper.'

The Coroner said he had put his question very carefully, did he buy it in a bottle or a package? – 'It was in a bottle and the bottle was in a packet.'

The Coroner turned to the jury and asked, 'Is there any doubt about the way I put the question?' and the foreman said dutifully that he had put it very plainly.

Walker said 'to the best of my recollection I used some of the cyanide to destroy wasps nests and later gave the rest to my foreman.'

The Coroner pointed out that in his first statement on May 26 Walker had told Burt and Spooner that three days after using the cyanide himself he had destroyed the bottle by putting it on his slow-combustion fire and that he did not give any to anyone else.

Walker said that was his recollection at the time. He agreed that he made a later statement, on June 15, that he had bought two lots of cyanide in the summer or autumn of 1937.

'I don't want to trap you in any way,' the Coroner said. 'Take as long as you like. Give your considered opinions.'

Walker hesitated and asked, almost to himself, 'Did I buy two lots in 1937?'

The Coroner nodded and repeated the question. Walker said lamely, 'I don't remember,'

The Coroner read in full from Walker's first statement that he may have bought some cyanide in 1936. He definitely bought some in July 1937 and later destroyed the bottle on the fire. He was certain that no-one else used the poison and Mrs Chandler would not have had access to any he had bought.

Wilson's voice took a harsher tone. 'That statement leaves no doubt at all in the minds of anyone that you personally used this cyanide which you bought in 1937 and yourself destroyed the bottle. Is that what you are saying quite plainly?' – 'That is what I say and at that time that was my recollection.'

'What now is your recollection?' – 'That it is now not correct.'

It took the Coroner six further questions to get Walker to admit that his statement was wrong in saying that only he had used the cyanide and that the bottle was kept in a place of safety before he had destroyed it.

The Coroner, 'It really comes to it that none of this statement is correct.' Walker nodded his head and agreed with him.

The Coroner then asked him why his evidence today varied from the statements he had made previously. 'Today I am upon oath,' Walker said.

The Coroner then went on to question Walker about Mrs Chandler's visits to Newmarket with Mr Murfitt, and sometimes with Mrs Murfitt as well. 'Was there ever in your mind any question of intimacy between Mr Murfitt and Mrs Chandler?' he asked. 'None,' replied Walker.

In answer to further questions, he also said that when he used Billy Murfitt's car he had not seen any keys similar to the front door key which the Coroner produced, and that he had never had in his possession any key which would fit the Murfitt's front door.

His evidence ended, Walker, looking tired, uncomfortable and distressed, walked to the back of the hall.

'Mary Elizabeth Fernie Chandler?' The Coroner checked the full name of his next witness, who had been waiting outside the hall since Walker started his evidence. Dressed in a blue costume, wide-brimmed black hat and clutching a small handbag, she strode confidently through the hall and took the chair in front of the Coroner. The reporters leaned forward to record every detail of her appearance and dress and waited for the questioning.

Wilson started quietly. He asked how she had met the Murfitts and how she had visited their home. He produced the tin of Fynnon Salts – had she ever noticed one of these tins on the sideboard? Never, she replied emphatically.

The Coroner then told her she was not obliged to answer any question which might incriminate her in connection with the fur coat case, asking her first if she had ever had in her possession a coat which she now understood was the property of Mrs Dawson Waugh. 'Yes', she replied. It came into her possession while she was at Newmarket with Mr Murfitt.

Did she know the police had taken statements from the Murfitts about the coat? Only after she came back from Scotland, she said. She had no idea how police came to learn about the coat being in her possession.

'Had you told Mrs Murfitt how it came into your possession? ' – 'No.'

Burt was amazed at her effrontery. Mrs Murfitt's version, which he had no cause to disbelieve, had been that Mrs Chandler had told her a friend in Scotland had asked her to sell it for her, and she had later introduced the housekeeper to a furrier in London.

The Coroner asked Mrs Chandler if she had ever had any quarrels with the Murfitts, had she got a grudge against either of them? 'Never at any time', she replied.

He then asked her the same question that he had put to Walker – was she in or near Murfitt's house between 8am on Monday,

May 16 and 9am on the Tuesday, the day he died? 'Never', she said.

'Was Mr Walker, as far as you know?' – 'No.'

'Can you say he could not have been there without your knowledge?' – 'He could have been there.'

'Could you have been there without his knowledge?' – 'No, because I was in bed.'

Burt made a note. Up to that time the Coroner, or anyone else as far as he knew, had not suggested the night time was a factor in the question. She seemed to have immediately assumed it.

The Coroner, 'I don't understand. Why does the fact that you were in bed make it impossible for you to be out without Mr Walker's knowledge? – 'He knew I was in bed when he went out and I was still in bed at lunchtime.'

'Well, what about the night? Could you have got up and gone out, or he got up and gone out, without each other's knowledge?' – 'No.'

'Why not?' – 'Because we were in each other's room.'

The Coroner queried her answer and Mrs Chandler explained, 'I mean he was in my room.' One or two gasps of surprise from those in the public seats and from previous witnesses who had stayed to listen. Walker looked embarrassed.

The Coroner then asked her about the Monday when, she said, she got up at ten minutes to one to have lunch. Walker was not there at that time, she said, and he would not have known what time she got up.

'So it really comes to this, neither Mr Walker can say what you were doing on Monday morning, nor can you say what Mr Walker was doing on Monday morning. Is that right?' – 'Yes.'

'And the same applies to the afternoon?' – 'Yes.'

'Either of you might have been in Mr Murfitt's house for all the other one knew?' – 'That might have happened.' She smiled as she said it, as if teasing the Coroner.

'But during the night it could not have happened because you were together in your bedroom?' – 'Yes.'

'Were you sleeping in the same bed?' – 'Yes.'

There were more gasps of astonishment at the frankness of her answers. The Bury Free Press reporter marked Mrs Chandler's reply that she and Walker were in the same bed with a question mark, because he wondered if the fact that unmarried people were sleeping together should be used in a family newspaper. (He was to find out later that the editor shared his doubt and cut that fact out.)

Burt exchanged glances with Spooner, who was filling his second notebook of the day. Dr Roche Lynch had estimated that the cyanide could not have been added to the salts before the Monday evening, and more probably during the night. Mrs Chandler's admission that she and Walker were in bed together at night gave them a strong alibi. And an alibi based on a sexual relationship, in this case probably near to a matrimonial relationship, would be almost impossible to disprove unless there was any independent evidence to the contrary.

The Coroner went on to ask Mrs Chandler whether she had ever had any cyanide of potassium in her possession. 'Never', she replied.

Had she ever seen any in the house? The first time was six or seven years ago, the last time the previous September. She had been with Walker when he had bought some of the poison in Bury St Edmunds in July and then in September he destroyed a wasps nest with it by emptying the bottle into a hole. She said she didn't know what he did with the bottle afterwards.

The Coroner, looking at her statement in front of him, asked her if she had told the detectives that after Walker destroyed the wasps nest she saw him put the bottle in the slow combustion stove and the melted glass came out 'just like a clinker.' She agreed she had said that.

The Coroner then asked if she had told the detectives that Walker always kept any cyanide in his safe in the pantry, the key of which he carried on a chain. How did she reconcile that with her evidence at the inquest that the cyanide bottle was kept on a chest in the cloakroom.

'When the police came to see me I was confused. I had been ill. I remembered afterwards,' she replied.

The Coroner then adjourned the hearing while Mrs Chandler read the statement she made to Burt and Spooner on June 15. When the hearing resumed he asked her if she wished to correct that statement. She said yes, she now wanted it to read that she did not know what Walker did with the bottle and that at least on one occasion she had seen a bottle on the chest in the cloakroom.

Questions about how Mrs Chandler wrote from Scotland to the maid, Joyce Middleditch, asking her to send her a bottle from Hall Farm did not seem to get the inquiry anywhere. Mrs Chandler told the Coroner that the bottle she asked for in the letter contained boracic crystals, but the maid wrote back that she could not find it.

Mrs Chandler denied that the maid also wrote that all she could find was some cyanide of potassium. The Coroner asked if, when she returned to the farm, she showed the maid a bottle labelled cyanide of potassium and said, 'That is the bottle I wished you to send.' She said she could not recollect saying that.

The Coroner queried why the housekeeper wanted the maid to send her 'a bottle of four-penny stuff' like boracic crystals when she could have bought it easily in Scotland. 'I wanted other things as well,' she replied.

The foreman of the jury then asked Mrs Chandler, 'I should like to know what you were doing on May 12, at ten o'clock at night?'

Mrs Chandler thought for a moment and replied that she had gone to Ipswich to have her hair done, had tea with Walker and then went to the cinema, getting home about 10.30pm.

The Coroner asked, 'If someone said they saw you outside Quays Farm between ten and ten thirty, walking, would there be any truth in it?' – 'Absolutely no.'

With Mrs Chandler's evidence at an end, the Coroner turned to the Chief Constable, who was sitting next to Burt and Superintendent Brinkley, and said, 'I think this is a suitable time to ask whether you intend to take proceedings against anyone at the moment, or whether you would like a short adjournment for the police to make further inquiries.'

Captain Robertson replied, 'There is no possibility at the moment of bringing any case against any person and the police would like an adjournment for 28 days, if possible, to make further inquiries.'

The Coroner then adjourned the inquest until Thursday, July 21st.

As they drove back to Bury St Edmunds, Burt and Spooner knew Walker and Mrs Chandler had lied throughout their evidence. Walker could not make his mind up when he bought cyanide and what he did with it, he gave the third version of the period he had known Mrs Chandler and they both lied about why they fell out with the Murfitts. Mrs Chandler had also changed her mind on what she told Mrs Murfitt about how she had come by the fur coat, and it was obvious that they had got together to put up that alibi of being in bed on the night of the 16th.

Their main hope now was that when the housekeeper appeared before West Suffolk Quarter Sessions in ten days time on the summons of receiving the fur coat some evidence might come out which would help their murder inquiries, but they knew it was a long shot.

Twenty Two **Fur coat case verdict**

Twenty Two

Fur coat case verdict

A BIG CROWD WAITED OUTSIDE the courthouse on the edge of the graveyard next to St James' Cathedral Church in Bury St Edmunds for the opening of the West Suffolk Quarter Sessions. From well before breakfast cars, some driven by uniformed chauffeurs, had been dropping elegantly dressed women and their escorts outside the court buildings and they stood on the steps, chattering away, waiting for the doors to open. Lawyers, famous names from London among them, pushed their way through the crowd and reporters moved forward trying to talk to them. Press photographers took pictures of everyone in sight, just in case.

Inside, chairs had been packed as tightly as possible in the public gallery while a gallery which had been closed for many years had been opened for the day to provide more seating. When the doors opened there was a scramble for seats and in the crush one woman fainted and was carried out by two policemen. The noise barely reduced when the door opened at the back of the court and the chairman, Sir Francis Dunnell, a local baronet, led in his full bench of nearly 30 magistrates, the largest complement they had had for some-time.

Fernie Chandler, pale and wearing a straw hat with a flowered dress under a three-quarter length brown coat, entered the court unseen by many as she walked to the dock. She looked slowly along the row of jurors, one of whom was a woman, while they were being sworn in and then smiled at her leading counsel, Mr John Flowers KC, her hands clasped tight to the dock rail. When the Clerk of the Peace read out the charge, that she received a lady's 175 guineas mink fur coat, the property of Mrs Edith Waugh, knowing very well it had been stolen, she pleaded not guilty in a low voice.

The defence team also included the barrister Mr Featherstone, who had represented Mrs Chandler at Newmarket, and a young barrister, Mr Boyd Carpenter, who was predicted to have a promising future in politics. (Many years later he was to become a Cabinet Minister.)

Mr Gerald Howard, a London barrister of high reputation instructed by the local firm of Bankes Ashton and Co., was prosecuting counsel. He outlined the case which had previously been put to the Newmarket magistrates, that Mrs Dawson Waugh, wife of the racehorse trainer, had missed the coat from her bedroom wardrobe on September 29, 1937, and that the coat was later sold by Mrs Chandler to a London furrier for £100, from where it had been recovered by police.

Mrs Chandler, he said, had told the police she had bought the coat for £60 from a woman at Newmarket racecourse when she was there with William Murfitt. The story, counsel said, was an improbable one and if they accepted as true the evidence they would hear from Mr Murfitt's chauffeur and from Mrs Murfitt, it was clear beyond all reasonable doubt that the house-keeper's story could not be believed.

Mrs Murfitt repeated the evidence she had given at Newmarket that Mrs Chandler had shown her the coat while she was visiting her at Hall Farm, and said she was selling it for a friend in Scotland. Later Mrs Chandler told her she had now bought the coat herself and Mrs Murfitt went with her to London, where she introduced Mrs Chandler to her furrier, who she learned later bought the coat.

The chauffeur, Ted Kydd, told the court that on the day Mrs Chandler said she bought the coat at the races he had driven to Newmarket town centre in the Ford Eight to meet Murfitt outside his club, the Subscription Rooms. They exchanged cars and Murfitt went into the club while Kydd drove Mrs Chandler home in the Buick. He did not see the coat in the car and when Mrs Chandler got out all she was carrying was a race card and a handbag.

Other witnesses gave identical evidence to that given to the Newmarket court to complete the case for the prosecution.

Mr Flowers submitted to the jury that the case against his client was extremely weak and he urged them to suspend their judgment until they had heard the whole of the evidence. This began when Mrs Chandler, accompanied by a woman court officer, walked from the dock to the witness box.

She told the court that when the chauffeur got into the car to drive her home she noticed that the fur coat, which she had put on the back seat, had fallen on to the floor. She picked it up and hung it over the handle of the door and when she got out at Risby she took the coat with her and hung it in the cloakroom.

The housekeeper said that when she showed the coat to James Walker he told her she had not been wise to buy it and asked how did she know it had not been stolen.

Mr Flowers intervened. 'It was not very wise, was it?' he said' – 'It certainly was not,' Mrs Chandler agreed.

The KC then asked why she had told Mrs Murfitt she had got the coat from a friend in Scotland. She replied, 'Purely because of Mr Walker's remark about the probability of the coat having been stolen. That was the only reason.'

Mrs Chandler's finances then came under close investigation. Mr Flowers, trying to put into the jury's minds that she had no reason to get involved in crime, asked her how much of her money she had in Mr Walker's safe. She had £180 in a cash box, she said.

Mr Howard rose and asked what salary she was paid. Mr Walker made her an annual allowance of £60, she said. 'Why doesn't he pay you a salary?' he asked, and added with a touch of malice, 'Why doesn't he pay you a salary as a housekeeper? Would you rather not answer that?' – 'It was not arranged as a salary,' she replied and Mr Howard left it at that.

Prosecuting counsel then scoffed at Mrs Chandler's statement that she had taken £40, more than half her yearly allowance, to Newmarket for one day's racing.

She replied that the £60 allowance was not her only income. Mr Walker gave her £10 for her birthday and the same at Christmas and she had the proceeds from the garden, the poultry and the egg money, all of which came to about £150 a year.

Mr Howard persisted. 'Are you accustomed to taking nearly one third of your annual income as a housekeeper and risking it on one day's racing? – 'I am accustomed to taking large sums of money about with me,' she replied.

'Why?' – 'Just habit,' adding that she believed that when she had large sums with her she was lucky.

The cross questioning carried on unmercifully but Mrs Chandler seemed to have an answer for everything. Why did she keep £180 in cash in Walker's safe? In case she needed it, she didn't like money in the bank. What was she likely to need it for? Anything, if she wished to go abroad, for example. Was she accustomed to going abroad at a day's notice? She had done once or twice, the last time a couple of years ago.

Mr Howard asked about her betting. Did she take £40 every time she went to the races? Not every time, it varied. On the day she bought the fur coat she said she had won £30 by winning the tote double. Mr Howard said, 'Fairly heavy betting for a housekeeper on £150 a year? – 'I don't think so,' replied Mrs Chandler. Had she ever bought a fur coat under these circumstances before? Never, she replied.

Everyone in the court was listening intently, fascinated by the details of a housekeeper's finances.

The questioning turned to the fur coat. It was October, said Mr Howard, yet this lady stripped off her fur coat and handed it over on a cold day? – 'She had a suit underneath.'

'Are you asking the jury to believe that you never asked this woman her name?' – 'I took her for a lady.'

Mrs Chandler said she did not get a receipt, nor did she take the woman's car number, adding 'It would have been wiser if I had done so.'

Why, asked Mr Howard, did she not mention buying the coat to Murfitt when he drove her from the racecourse to his club in Newmarket? – 'Mr Murfitt was discussing a private matter with me.' She didn't say what that matter was and Mr Howard said he didn't want to go into it, leaving an air of mystery over that stage of the cross-examination.

Mr Howard came back again to his point, 'Here you are doing a very odd and unusual transaction and it is actually put into Mr Murfitt's car, yet you don't say a word to him about it? – 'I intended telling Mr Murfitt.'

'Why didn't you?' – 'Mr Murfitt got into the car and we discussed another matter.'

How about when she drove home with the chauffeur, asked Mr Howard. Just how did she put the coat on the handle of the car door? – 'I just hung it up by the collar.'

'The nearside door was open, wasn't it, because you had just got out?' – 'I shut the door.'

'I am bound to suggest to you that it never happened.' – ' That is quite wrong.'

Now what about the chauffeur's evidence that she did not carry the fur coat out of the car when they reached Hall Farm, asked Mr Howard. He had said all she was carrying was a race card and a bag. – 'That is quite untrue,' replied Mrs Chandler. 'I did carry the coat.'

When did she realise the coat might have been stolen, asked Mr Howard. Sometime after Mr Walker had suggested it was a possibility, she replied. Mr Howard asked if she took any steps to find out if the coat was stolen. No, she said, and she did not know why she hadn't.

She first told Mrs Murfitt she was selling the coat for a friend in Scotland, and later said she had bought the coat from that friend. Were those lies? Yes, admitted Mrs Chandler.

With the end of her evidence, the chairman adjourned the hearing for lunch. Some of the ladies in the public gallery stayed in their seats in case they would not be able to get in again. At least one had brought sandwiches.

After the break the next witness was James Walker, who told how he came into the house at about six o'clock on the evening that Mrs Chandler returned from the races and noticed the strange fur coat in the cloakroom. At first he thought they had a visitor and asked Mrs Chandler who was in the house. She then told him that she had bought the coat at the races and he asked if she had been wise doing that. But after going into the matter with her so thoroughly, he said, she so impressed his mind that he had no further doubt.

Mr Flowers asked what happened when Mrs Chandler took money from the box in the pantry. He said he asked her, 'Why take so much money? You will lose it?' and she replied, 'No, I have never lost it yet. Money brings me luck.'

Mr Howard rose again, with the intention of wrong-footing Walker even on small details. Where was the coat hanging when he came in? In the cloakroom, Walker said. Yet he told Inspector Butcher that it was hanging in the hall. – 'I meant the cloakroom, there is no peg in the hall,' Walker said.

Had Mrs Chandler told him that the woman she bought the coat from had come down from Scotland? – 'I cannot remember'

'Well try to think, Mr Walker.'

After a pause Walker replied, 'Yes,'

'She never said a word about that in her evidence today. Did she tell you that? – 'That is what I believe.'

Walker also said that when Mrs Murfitt said Mrs Chandler told her the coat was lent to her by a friend in Scotland he realised the housekeeper had been telling a lie. Walker again looked nervous and distressed as he ended his evidence.

Mr Flowers then rose to address the jury, saying that if the explanation given by Mrs Chandler could be reasonably true, then she was entitled to be acquitted. 'What she did was unwise, goodness knows the folly of it, but folly is not a crime,' he said. 'Taking a fair view of the evidence, I say it falls far short of the standard of proof which, fortunately, we demand in this country before a person is convicted in a criminal court.'

After Mr Howard had submitted that the prosecution had proved its case, and the chairman had summed up the evidence, the jury filed out to consider their verdict. It took them two hours and there were some gasps of surprise when the foreman, asked for their decision, announced, 'Not guilty.'

Mr Howard, his assistants and the police began an animated conversation. The Dawson Waughs looked glum. The bench of 30 magistrates filed out, thinking it was one of the most interesting days they had experienced.

Outside the court Mrs Chandler and her barrister, Mr Featherstone, were surrounded by reporters as the photographers' flashguns went off. 'No, I was not anxious,' she told the Pressmen. 'I had a Scotswoman's intuition that my innocence would be proved in the end.' And with that she was driven off.

The rear entrance of Quays Farm in 1938

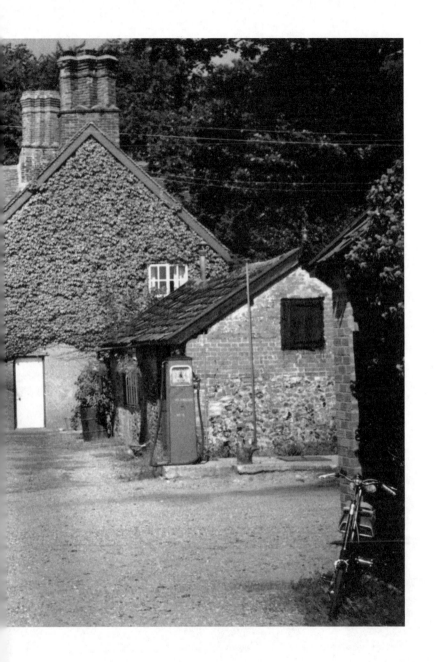

Twenty Three **'An extremely cunning woman'**

Twenty Three
'An extremely cunning woman'

Burt's report reveals two important points that could not be revealed to the jury in the fur coat case that, had they been aware of them, would almost certainly have caused them to find Mrs Chandler guilty and in all probability for her to be sent to jail. One was the contents of Bill Murfitt's statement about what happened at Newmarket races, evidence which could not be put before the court because he was dead. The other was Mrs Chandler's previous criminal record for stealing a fur coat before she moved to Risby.

AFTER POLICE RECOVERED EDITH WAUGH'S mink coat from the furrier's, and Mrs Chandler had given her explanation that she had bought the coat from a woman a Newmarket races, they interviewed Bill Murfitt. A month before he died he made a statement to Inspector Butcher which said, 'On a day in October last year, I cannot say the day except it was a race day at Newmarket, Mrs Chandler asked me if she could go to Newmarket races with me, and she did so. When we arrived we went to the paddock. I saw her at frequent intervals during the races, to the best of my knowledge we went back to the car together after the races. My car I always lock when I leave it on the course, and it would not have been possible for anyone to have placed anything on the seats of the car. Mrs Chandler did not say anything to me about buying a fur coat, and I did not see a coat in the car. Upon arriving at my club in Newmarket I met my man Kydd, who had brought my small car over. He drove Mrs Chandler home in the car we left the course with. I distinctly remember she was wearing a musquash fur coat that day.'

Because Murfitt was now dead that statement could not be used by the prosecution in the fur coat case.

There was another important piece of information that could, if the prosecution had been allowed to produce it in court, have had a major influence both on the magistrates at Newmarket, who cleared Mrs Chandler on the theft charge, and on the jury at quarter sessions, who had just acquitted her on the receiving charge.

In this case, what the jury did not know was that when Mrs Chandler – or Lady Fernie, or Lady Mary as she variously called herself – was living in London in 1924 she booked into the

Albany Hotel in Lancaster Gate for a few days. Just as she was about to book out, police stopped her and asked if they could inspect her luggage. Protruding from one of her boxes was a fur coat and on inspection it turned out to be a musquash which another resident had reported missing from her room.

Mrs Chandler gave no trouble, confessed to the theft and on October 11 that year the Marylebone magistrate, noting that she had pleaded guilty and that it was her first offence (the first that had come to court, at least) bound her over for two years for £50, the sum she would have to pay if she transgressed again in that period.

When, at Hall Farm, Risby on June 8, 1938, West Suffolk police charged her with the theft and the receiving of Mrs Waugh's fur coat, they also put to her the 1924 Marylebone conviction, which she admitted. Walker, who was also in the room, told the officers he was aware of the conviction because he knew Mrs Chandler at the time she was charged, in fact two years before she came to work for him at Risby.

Evidence about the earlier conviction could not be given at the petty sessions or quarter sessions because, except in special cases, details of a defendant's previous criminal record can only be divulged after the accused person is found guilty, in case magistrates or a jury should be prejudiced against the defendant by that knowledge.

Although the young chauffeur, Ted Kydd, had given evidence that he did not see the coat in the car when he drove Mrs Chandler home from Newmarket, it did not bear too heavily on the jury, perhaps because of his age and position. If Murfitt had been able to give his evidence that Mrs Chandler could not have put the mink into his Buick because it was locked, this would have demolished Mrs Chandler's alibi and she would almost certainly have been found guilty.

If a guilty verdict had been returned the prosecution would then have been able put Mrs Chandler's previous conviction before the court so that it could be taken into consideration when sentence was being considered. In those circumstances, for a second similar conviction, there was a good chance she would have been sent to jail. That, to Burt, seemed a strong enough motive for Mrs Chandler to make sure Murfitt was out of the way before she appeared in court. But soon after her acquittal he was to learn she had an even stronger motive, one involving money.

Since the adjournment of the inquest on June 25 Burt and Spooner increased their inquiries among personal friends of Walker and Chandler to try and find some explanation for Walker's behaviour. Burt wrote in his report, 'It seemed unlikely (although certainly possible) that he was responsible for Murfitt's death, but it did seem reasonable to conjecture that he was doing all he could to relieve Mrs Chandler of suspicion in the matter and in the process of doing so had compromised himself.' Burt also made sure Walker knew of the inquiries they were making about him.

As a result of the pressure being put upon him, Walker called at Bury St Edmunds police station two days after the fur coat case and asked to see the Chief Inspector. 'He said he had been a fool and wished now to be open and frank with me and tell me all he knew,' Burt wrote.

Walker talked about himself and Mrs Chandler and said he now knew more about her character than he did before, but Burt noted that whenever he tried to discuss anything related to Murfitt's death the farmer said he did not know or could not remember, although he wished he could. 'I gained the impression that although Walker was being truthful in many respects and was endeavouring to redeem himself, he was still reticent in regard to certain matters in which I thought he could assist me in my investigations,' Burt noted.

Walker told Burt that because of what he now knew about Mrs Chandler he had told her she must leave his house but, upset by this, she was now confined to bed and was being attended by the doctor. She had also taken a bottle of laudanum from his cupboard and he feared she may take her own life with the drug.

Walker did not give much more information and Burt wondered why he had called. Mrs Chandler, it transpired, heard that her employer had called to see the detective and immediately called in her solicitors from London, apparently, Burt thought, because she feared he would compromise her in some way. Two solicitors arrived at Hall Farm the same day and soon afterwards Mrs Chandler was taken to a nursing home at Cambridge.

Five days after Walker called at the police station Burt and Spooner visited him at Hall Farm. He was in much the same state as when Burt had last seen him, greatly distressed by his deception by Mrs Chandler and angry at the way he had been disgraced in the eyes of his friends.

He told Burt he had been blind to things he should have seen and recalled a warning he had been given a long time before by Superintendent Brinkley, about his housekeeper's suspected criminal activities. He just did not believe it at the time, he said.

'I have been a fool and a cad to my friends,' he said over and over again, and referred to people to whose homes he had introduced Mrs Chandler to and who had been the victims of thefts. 'I have been thoroughly deceived by that woman,' he told the detectives.

Burt was cautious. He remembered earlier interviews when Walker had deliberately tried to mislead them but gradually he began to believe that Walker now genuinely wanted to help them. Burt knew that Mrs Chandler had a motive for poisoning Murfitt by stopping him giving evidence against her in the fur coat trial, but he thought there might be more to it than at first appeared.

The detective noted, 'I therefore very carefully questioned Walker to see if another possible motive which had been apparent to me was supported by any evidence of fact. The information I thus obtained is, in my submission, of considerable importance.'

The story which Walker gave him made it clear just how gullible he was as far as his housekeeper was concerned. When he questioned her in Scotland about how she acquired the mink he was completely taken in by her story of innocence. He was so convinced that he decided to stand by her and, he said, immediately made a will leaving everything he owned to her. Although he was not wealthy at the time, he was due to inherit about £6,000 on the death of his elderly mother, a considerable sum in 1938, and as Mrs Chandler was 20 years younger than he was she would have a lot to gain when he died. It followed that she would also have had a lot to lose if Murfitt's evidence had been given in the fur coat case and she had been found guilty and sent to jail, because it was then highly probable that Walker would consider himself shamed in public and would cut her out of his will.

Burt wrote of the interview with Walker, 'It seems almost incomprehensible that a man of Walker's undoubted education and intelligence should have been guiled to the extent that he has been... there is no doubt that he was associated with an extremely cunning woman.'

The detective had other questions for Walker. What was the truth about how long he had known Mrs Chandler, for instance? Walker said he had first met her in December, 1926, six months after his wife died. Because he was lonely after her death he answered an advertisement she had put in The Scotsman newspaper offering her services as a housekeeper. Burt asked him why he had told both himself and the Coroner he had known Mrs Chandler longer than that, and he said he thought it looked better for her sake.

Burt, who thought Mrs Chandler's alibi that they slept in the same bed on the night before Murfitt's murder was too coincidental, asked if this was true. Walker replied that they had slept together for a long time and did so on that night.

It was when Burt asked him questions about the use of cyanide and about the movements of him and Mrs Chandler at the time of the murder that the farmer became confused and muddled, and the detective formed the opinion that he was not telling the truth. Burt noted that it was obvious that Walker suspected Mrs Chandler of poisoning Murfitt and this had possibly affected him in such a way that he could not think clearly.

When he asked Walker if he was prepared to make a statement about what he had just told him the farmer said his solicitors had advised him not to make any other statement at present. Burt was stymied once again.

While they were at Hall Farm, Burt took the opportunity to get local police to search the premises and the farmer offered no objection. They searched all the rooms in the house, the gardens and the farmyard, and a small meadow at the side of the house. Burt himself paid particular attention to a bin in which cinders and ash from the slow combustion Aga stove were deposited. All this time Walker was completely co-operative with the searchers, opening cupboard doors, suggesting places where they might like to look next. While Spooner was searching the bedrooms he came across Mrs Chandler's clothes and other effects packed in trunks ready for removal and meticulously went through them. At the end of the day they found nothing which would help their investigations.

• •

That evening, unknown to Burt and Spooner while they were driving back to Bury St Edmunds, a lone woman passenger carrying a small suitcase got off the Cambridge train at Saxham and Risby station. She walked the hundred or so yards to the A45, turned to her left and walked along the grass verge beside the turnpike until she came to the top of South Street which led into the village.

By the time she reached Hall Farm, after a two-mile walk on a warm summer evening, the woman, although smartly dressed, was hot, dusty and dishevelled. Her ringing of the door bell was answered by a maid, who then went inside again. James Walker appeared and there was an animated conversion on the doorstep before he stepped aside to let the woman in.

Not long afterwards Walker and the woman left the house and got into Walker's car. The staff, peering from the side of a window, noticed she was crying. Half an hour later, when the car drew up outside a nursing home in Cambridge, she was still crying. Fernie Chandler had gone to Risby and pleaded to be taken back, and had been refused by her former employer.

Twenty Four **Inquest verdict –
murderer unknown**

Twenty Four
Inquest verdict –
murderer unknown

RISBY VILLAGE HALL WAS AGAIN full when the inquest on William Murfitt resumed on Thursday, July 21, just over nine weeks after his death. The reporters, who in the month since the previous hearing had forsaken the village for sensations elsewhere, were back with their photographers, and villagers and others from outside queued again at the door hoping to get seats. All the witnesses who had given evidence at the previous hearing were there and were allowed to sit in the hall. They included Mrs Murfitt, still in widow's black but with a few more white trimmings than before, sitting with her two sons, Leslie and Billy, her daughter-in-law Ricky and her sister Emma Ruston. The Chief Constable and his deputy sat with Burt and Spooner, and Sergeants Willis and Bigmore, the two mainstays of the searches that had gone on all summer, sat in chairs behind them.

Thomas Wilson, the Coroner, who had on his list only four witnesses to be called that day unless something unexpected occurred, thought he might be home by lunchtime. In opening the hearing he asked what legal representatives were present and the barrister, Mr Featherstone, recalled the previous hearing when he had announced that he had been asked to watch the proceedings, but that it had not been necessary for him to disclose who he had been instructed by. At that hearing, he said, he had been there representing Mr Walker and Mrs Chandler but now he wished to say that at his hearing he represented only Mrs Chandler.

Furthermore, he said, he had a medical certificate regarding the health of Mrs Chandler, who had been in a nursing home in Cambridge for the past fortnight. She was at the inquest today, accompanied by a matron from the home, and he was making an application that she be allowed to return there at the earliest opportunity. 'I would ask you, if she is not to be recalled today, that she can leave the court now. I can hand in the doctor's certificate,' he said.

The Coroner, who knew of Mrs Chandler's train journey to Hall Farm nine days earlier, replied tartly, 'That may be so, but I happen to know that she has been over here unattended some time quite recently. I do not expect it will be necessary to call Mrs Chandler very long, but I do not think I can say at this stage that I shall not ask her any further questions.'

Mr Featherstone sat down and motioned to a clerk behind him, who went out to convey the news to Mrs Chandler, who was sitting in a car parked on the side of the road accompanied by the matron. Walker, sitting in his car parked on the other side of the road, wondered what development had taken place.

The inquest continued with another barrister, Mr Alban Gordon, saying that he now represented Mr Walker and Thomas Ashton said he was representing the Murfitt family.

The first witness, Violet Middleditch, said she had been a domestic servant at Hall Farm until October 2, and she related the story of how in the August Mrs Chandler had written from Scotland asking her to send a bottle which she would find in a bench in the cloakroom. The only bottle she could find, Miss Middleditch said, was on the cloakroom floor, it was dark green, two or three inches high and was labelled 'Poison, Cyanide'. She did not send the bottle to Mrs Chandler because she did not think it was the one she required. There was little new in her evidence and the Press table began to yawn.

The milk boy, Will Ashman, to whom Miss Middleditch had shown the bottle, said in evidence that Mr Walker had given him a similar one when, in September, he asked him for some cyanide to destroy a wasps nest. He used up all the contents and left the bottle in the tree stump where the wasps nest was.

The only real interest in the proceedings so far had been while Miss Middleditch had been giving evidence and Elaine Browne had entered the hall, accompanied by her husband who had to support her by holding her arm. She looked very ill and was allowed into a small room at the back of the hall where she was given a glass of water.

When she was called to the witnesses' chair she was again helped by her husband, who was obviously upset. He turned angrily to the Coroner and said, 'You never gave me a moment's notice you desired Mrs Browne to come here today, sir. She has been under the doctor, you might have given her some consideration.'

The Coroner, unmoved, made no comment. He asked Mrs Browne about her friendship with the Murfitts and where she had been the day before he died. She had been to London, returning about 7.30pm, she said, she went to bed about 9.30 and did not get up during the night. Even when the Coroner asked her about her adulterous relationship with Murfitt there was little interest shown on the Press table as they had heard it all before. At the end of her evidence she was allowed to leave and returned to Fornham with her husband.

The Coroner then told Mr Featherstone he did not think any useful purpose would be served by recalling Mrs Chandler as a witness and that she could leave if she wanted to. The clerk went out to the car where she was still sitting and she was driven off by the matron while James Walker, still in his car on the other side of the road, looked on.

In his summing up, Thomas Wilson told the jury they could rest assured no stone had been left unturned in trying to get to the bottom of this case. Sergeants Willis and Bigmore, with the memory of long searches in hedges, fields, ponds and buildings galore still in their minds, nodded in earnest agreement. The Coroner said there were three alternatives open to the jury, that Mr Murfitt had taken the poison accidentally, that he had deliberately taken it to take his own life, or that someone had deliberately put the poison in the health salts. He discounted the possibilities of accident or suicide and for the verdict of murder they had to consider motive and opportunity.

He discussed the relationship between Mr and Mrs Murfitt and said at the time of his death it was better than it had been at any time of their married life. Murfitt's relationship with Mrs Browne had been forgiven and the jury had been told that Mrs Murfitt had drawn attention to the condition of the salts and that ruled her out as the poisoner.

The Coroner took some time discussing the possibility that the poison was put in the salts to kill either Mr or Mrs Murfitt or both, because a person who knew Mr Murfitt took salts was quite likely to know that Mrs Murfitt did also. Then he turned to the question of Murfitt and Mrs Browne, saying that if Mr Browne had known suddenly of their improper relationship it was conceivable that he might have wished to do Murfitt serious injury.

'But he did not seem to be the sort of person who would get his own back on a man who had done him serious injury by poisoning,' he said. 'It is much more likely he would give the man a good hiding, or take proceedings against his wife and claim damages against the man if he could.'

He then turned to the 'discrepancy of evidence' given by Walker and his housekeeper, and left little doubt as to what he thought of them as witnesses. 'What credence are we to give to their evidence?' he asked the jury. 'I don't suppose it wants words of mine to remind you of the way in which their evidence was given, the way in which they first said one thing and then another. There were various statements made to the police which varied from one another and also varied from the material particulars of the evidence given on oath.'

Motives? With regard to Mrs Chandler, the Coroner said she had reason to believe she would be charged with stealing or receiving a fur coat, an offence for which she would be extremely lucky if she had not been sent to a short sentence of penal servitude if convicted, but she was in fact acquitted. It seemed hard to believe, though, that anybody, to avoid the possibility of a sentence of imprisonment, would commit murder.

At the end of his summing up the Coroner referred to the fact that it was apparent Mrs Chandler knew that statements had been taken from the Murfitts and that both were likely to give evidence in the fur coat case. He then threw this closing thought to the jury, 'There was a motive, but how much it weighed with Mrs Chandler cannot be said,'

Burt wondered if his conversation with Walker about the will, which could not be given in evidence because the farmer had refused to commit it to a sworn statement, had been passed on privately to Thomas Wilson by the Chief Constable, with whom he had discussed it.

The jury filed into one of the small rooms at the back of the hall to consider their verdict. The Coroner retired to the other small room for a cup of tea. Spooner went out for a smoke followed by a group of reporters. Mr Featherstone and Thomas Ashton talked together in the detached way lawyers on opposite sides tend to do after a case. Chief Inspector Leonard Burt sat still in his seat, his face immobile, not hearing any of the buzz of conversation going on around him.

It took the jury just half an hour to consider their verdict and the foreman announced it to the Coroner – 'Murder against some person or persons unknown.'

Burt knew that unless things changed considerably, especially the attitude of James Walker, that was as good as he was going to get.

• •

The resumed inquest hearing had taken just three hours, and by the time Syd Williams had returned from the village hall to Quays Farm to check on a delivery and then cycle home for a late lunch there was already a crowd of reporters and photographers waiting round the foreman's front gate. They had already been given short shrift by the Murfitts and they were looking for anyone with a connection with the family who might give them a revealing quote.

'Syd, can we have a word?... Mr Williams, over here for a minute... Syd, what can you tell us about the Murfitts?' The reporters spilled through the gate on to the small flower bed and piece of lawn which his wife Rose had carefully cultivated. He could see her looking out anxiously from the front room window. Syd had been told by Burt to be wary about what he said to anyone about the case, especially the Press.

One reporter sidled up close to him and whispered, 'Can we have a chat up at the pub tonight as soon as they open. There could be something in it for you.' Although the thought of a few bob on the side initially appealed to him, Syd knew he had to be careful.

Standing on the edge of the crowd of reporters Syd had seen Frank Williams, the Bury reporter for the East Anglian Daily Times which was published from Ipswich. Frank was his cousin and although he didn't see him very often, they occasionally bumped into each other at the Wednesday cattle market. The idea of pursuing witnesses to their homes was alien to Frank's normal way of working, but he was on the books of most of the national papers as an accredited correspondent for the Bury area and he had received telephone calls that afternoon from some of the London news-desks asking him to keep a watch on the inquest.

Syd walked over to Frank, took him to one side and asked. 'What do you think I should I do?' Frank replied: 'It's up to you, but if I were you I wouldn't say a word, but don't tell these buggers I told you so.' As Syd turned away Frank added quietly, 'But if you learn anything new you know where my office is.'

That night three or four of the reporters waited outside the Crown and Castle as it opened at seven o'clock but Syd Williams didn't turn up. He told his wife, 'Those reporters want to get me drunk and see if I will say anything.' So, at his usual time of around eight o'clock, instead of going to the Crown and Castle for a drink he cycled two miles in the other direction to the Greyhound at Flempton. In Risby the reporters became tired of waiting and went into the pub for a farewell drink.

Twenty Five **Mrs Chandler sells her story**

Twenty Five
Mrs Chandler sells her story

Burt's increasing frustration at not being able to find the missing link of evidence which stopped him being able to prosecute Mrs Chandler for murder is reflected in his report. He knew she had a strong motive – to stop Murfitt giving evidence against her, which would have put her at grave risk of being sent to jail and denied her the chance of inheriting Walker's money. Indeed, as she knew the habits of the Murfitts well, she might have thought she could poison Gertrude at the same time and stop her evidence going before the court as well.

The timing of events pointed clearly to the housekeeper as the poisoner. By the middle of April the fur coat had been traced to the furriers in London, Mrs Chandler and Walker had been interviewed in Scotland and Walker had made his will in her favour. On April 20th Bill and Gertrude Murfitt gave their statements to the police on the fur coat case and Mrs Chandler would have known how much their evidence was likely to cost her. In the days after that a woman identified almost certainly as Mrs Chandler was seen by Murfitt's employees walking alone near Quays Farm at night – were these rehearsals for the final journey to the dining room on May 17 or was she scared off on both occasions because she knew she had been seen? Mrs Chandler's proven talent for getting into other people's houses unseen fitted her well for the crime.

The vital missing evidence was proof that she had actually entered the farmhouse in the hours just before Murfitt died to put the cyanide salts in the tin. Burt knew, if only to satisfy himself, that before he left Bury St Edmunds he had to prove that the housekeeper had the opportunity to do so.

On the Thursday following the inquest verdict the detective drove alone to Risby at night and parked his car well away from Hall Farm before quietly making his way to Walker's back garden. He walked slowly across the lawn, through a small gate at the end of the garden and out into a meadow. It was well after ten o'clock on a night when clouds completely obscured the moon and the only visible light was from one of the bedroom windows in Hall Farm. He walked along a footpath, a thick hedge and large trees hiding a farmhouse called Charman's, the third manor house which, with Hall Farm and Quays Farm, had made up the original village.

At the end of the footpath was a stile about four feet high leading on to the road. Burt climbed over the stile and walked through long grass to stand on the road's edge, pausing for a while to check if anyone else was about and, turning left, walked towards Quays Farm, keeping on the grass verge to avoid making a noise. Risby, with no electricity and therefore no street lights, was in complete darkness. There was no reflection on the pond outside Charman's, just the splash of a moorhen briefly disturbed, and ahead another pond with railings round it which stopped opposite the farm entrance to the Murfitt's property.

The detective crossed to the right hand side of the road, walked through some farm buildings and came out a few yards away from the front gate of the farmhouse. He lifted the gate latch, walked the few steps to the front door and opened it with a key he'd brought with him. Burt moved silently to the right into the dining room and stood for a few seconds in the darkness near the sideboard before leaving the room. He closed the front door and walked down the short path on to the road, returning along the same route to Hall Farm, which was now in complete darkness.

As he quietly closed Walker's garden gate behind him and strode once more across the meadow towards his car, Burt took a small torch from his pocket and shone it on his wrist watch. The walk from Hall Farm to Quays Farm and back had taken him just ten minutes. He had seen no-one and no-one had seen him, for in Risby, once the last drinkers had left the Crown and Castle just after ten o'clock closing time and made their unsteady way home, there were few people about. It was the same walk that Mrs Chandler could easily have taken late on May 16th, or early the next morning, and it was possible that Walker, even if he had been sleeping in the same bed as his housekeeper, might not have known about it.

Burt returned to the Suffolk Hotel in Bury St Edmunds. The reporters and photographers had left at the weekend, their story over. Burt intended to clear his desk at Bury police station the next day and leave local police to carry on the investigations.

• •

The Empire News was a Sunday newspaper which covered some serious news, but not much. The August Bank Holiday edition informed its readers that Mussolini had rejected a plea from the Pope not to follow Hitler in his anti-Semitism policies. Another story reported that the German public would not be allowed to see the film of the fight in which the American black boxer Joe Louis battered the German Max Schmeling – 'for moral reasons' it was said in Germany. Sport had wide coverage, with a cricket league table showing Donald Bradman at the top with an average of 123 per innings and a story how a young Denis Compton might not be able to go on the South African cricket tour in the winter, because he was under contract as a professional footballer to Arsenal.

However, in the Empire News that Sunday, ten days after the inquest verdict, the main story appeared under the name of Mrs Mary Elizabeth Chandler with a Page One headline saying 'My Private Talks with Bill Murfitt' and a sub heading 'Women and Suicide'. A picture of a smiling Mrs Chandler – 'in happier days' said the caption underneath – appeared at the top of a story telling, in the hyperbolical style of a journalist ghost writer, of her pain and anguish at the treatment she had received as a result of recent events, 'circumstances,' she said, 'which compel me to break my self-imposed silence.'

In it, for a good fee, Mrs Chandler complained, 'I have been a much-maligned woman; in the stocks of wicked gossip. It has been said that I rob sparrows' nests, pull the heads off the young ones and trample on their bodies. Can evil imagination go further? People who know me will tell you that I cannot suffer to see a chicken killed.' She was quoted as saying that the accusation by gossips that she had poisoned William Murfitt had brought about 'an edifice of condemnation in which they incarcerated me... a target was needed for their poison missiles and I was that target.'

She continued in like manner, 'Matters which I thought were known of by the police only were public fodder, topics of telephone talks. I became, in evil gossip, a thief, a sadist, a receiver and a poisoner. My private life, of which I am forced here to tell, was ribboned by the lancet-like tongues that dissected it.' She was grateful that the magistrates and the jury she had faced, 'deafened their ears to unsupported calumny, blinded their eyes to accusative gesture.'

The main thrust of the article was to explain why, on the day she said she bought the fur coat at Newmarket races, she did not discuss the matter with Murfitt on their car ride to his club. She did not say at the trial what subject they did discuss but now, in her own defence, she want to reveal for the first time what it was.

After the races, she said, Mr Murfitt was gloomy. 'No sooner had he got to the wheel of the car than his temper broke,' her article stated. 'He had been thinking, it was evident, about one of the women with whom he had been intimately associated.'

Murfitt told her, 'I feel I could put a bullet through my brain.' She asked him why and he replied that although he was trying to keep women out of his life, circumstances which he could not control were working against him.

According to the article, Murfitt said one woman had had lots of money from him and he was not going to fall for any black-mail, so that it was useless her trying to crash into his life again. 'At that time he had foresworn women with his customary declamations of the sex, worded so as to include touches of profanity,' the article continued.

Mrs Chandler, or her ghost writer, wrote that Murfitt told her that one of his women had caused him no end of trouble and expense, and had said she wanted his wife to divorce him so that she could be free to marry him. 'Murfitt was furious about this. As I have stated, with all his weaknesses and personal criticisms, he would never allow anyone to challenge the rights of his wife.' She went on, 'With one of his loves out of his life and another taboo, Murfitt, I firmly believe, became mentally disturbed and in that state of disturbance he began to talk of suicide.'

Then, in the lurid language with which the article is peppered, Mrs Chandler says of the 'wicked lies' of her accusers, 'If it has permanently separated me from my friends, I suppose my enemies, whoever they may be – and until this breach I did not know I had any – will feel victorious.' Obviously referring to Walker, she continued, 'Let them know, too, that I dearly loved, and still dearly love, the man they have apparently suc-ceeded in turning against me after eleven years of mutual devotion. It is the crowning tragedy in a life that has not been free from tragedy through no fault of my own.' She added,

'The wings on which I felt I was gliding through life were torn from me and I was dashed down to disappointment and despair.'

Mrs Chandler's 'revelations' ran to some 3,500 words that week, and at the end the Empire News promised its readers that it would continue 'this remarkable story' in its next edition.

• •

The Empire News edition of August 7th told of Mrs Chandler's humble beginnings, her journey to India as nurse-governess to a wealthy family and her marriage to Mr Chandler, who was much older than her and had a daughter of 15. 'I had servants galore, a magnificent house (a picture of a magnificent Indian house illustrated the article), my own car and an allowance that provided amply for my needs.'

All this, it appeared, was spoilt by two factors – she could not get on with her new step-daughter, who considered her an interloper, and her husband who, although loving her devotedly, made no allowance for their difference in age. 'He did not appreciate how close to tyranny was his desire to have me always about the home and placing limitations on my freedom, which upset my whole nervous system.'

Her husband, she said, paid for her passage home and gave her an ample allowance in the hope that after a change of scene she would return. But she now wanted a divorce and although Mr Chandler would not agree to one she was advised that her only course was to do something to disgrace herself so much in his eyes that he would set her free.

That, she told her readers, was how she at one time came to be known as Lady Mary Chandler and how she became involved in the 1924 case of the first fur coat which, because she was found not guilty at the Bury St Edmunds trial, the police were unable to put before the court.

It described in the article how, on her return to London in 1924, she found a friend, whom she called The Jester, who jokingly introduced her to others as Lady Mary. The Jester recommended her a hotel and one day a box unexpectedly appeared in her room. Inside it she found a fur coat. She thought it had been left there by mistake by a maid or page, and as she was in a hurry to go out that evening, she put the coat in her own box for safety.

When she returned later that night, she wrote, she found two policemen had been into her room, searched her luggage and found the fur coat – and that was the chance she had been waiting for. She allowed the police to believe she intended stealing the coat and told them she was prepared to accept the consequences. After she appeared in court and was found guilty a newspaper published a paragraph about the case and, hoping this was disgrace enough, she sent the cutting to Mr Chandler in India. Unfortunately he forgave her and advised her to take the next boat back to India. Instead, she went back to Scotland hoping to find a post and it was through her advertisement in a newspaper that she met Mr Walker and became his housekeeper.

She finished the article with an attack upon her 'slanderers'. 'They have sundered the friendship between Mr Walker and myself; they have ejected me from my home into a world in which evil tongues have tried to make it impossible for me to live. I have nothing but hope – hope that someone will offer me a job.'

At the bottom of the page, adjoining the article, was an advertisement showing a healthy-looking old salt saying how grateful he was for a 'wonderful new joy in life', accompanied by a headline saying 'It's the Little Daily Dose that does it!' The advertisement was for Kruschen Salts, the benefits of which Murfitt had forsaken just before his death for their deadly rivals Fynnon.

Twenty Six   **'A wicked criminal…
an unmitigated liar'**

Twenty Six
'A wicked criminal... an unmitigated liar'

Just over a week after Burt had returned to London he received a telephone call from a Mr Tate of the London legal firm of Spiro and Co. saying that Walker would like to make another statement, adding that he hoped this would end the continual visits and questions he was having to deal with from the Bury police.

Burt took Spooner with him to the meeting on August 13th and when they met Walker in his solicitor's office they noticed he looked pale and drawn and appeared to have lost weight. Although Walker gave the impression that he wanted to help, there was little new at first in the information he gave them.

Burt, however, did get him talking and eventually Walker revealed that on the day of the theft of the fur coat in September, 1937, he and Mrs Chandler were in Bury St Edmunds, where his car was parked outside a hairdresser's shop. He agreed with Mrs Chandler's request to borrow the car, to visit a friend in the West Suffolk Hospital in Bury she said, and she was back after about half-an-hour at four o'clock.

Burt worked it out that if that half-an-hour had in fact been 45 minutes which, knowing Walker's ability to confuse or lie it could well have been, Mrs Chandler would have had time to have driven the car to Mrs Waugh's house in Newmarket, walked in and stolen the coat and returned to Bury St Edmunds.

When they began talking about Walker's will the farmer once again changed his story. This time he said he had made a will in favour of Mrs Chandler some years previously, but when he visited her in Scotland in April he had made another will to assure her of his faith in her, but that it was not done through a solicitor. He did, however, confirm that he had now made a new will disinheriting her.

Three days after that meeting Burt received a telephone call from a Mr Fruitman, a solicitor now acting for Mrs Chandler, saying he was trying to trace her husband, whom she left behind in India, and asking for any help Burt could give. Burt went to see him in his office in Chancery Lane but Burt noted that it soon became apparent that the real reason the solicitor has contacted him was to try to find what evidence the police had against his client.

Mr Fruitman told Burt that Mrs Chandler had received money from the Empire News newspaper for the articles they published under her name, and he wanted to know what the chances were of her being charged with murder so that, if necessary, provision could be made to pay for her defence.

Mr Fruitman also told Burt there was little hope of a reconciliation between Mrs Chandler and Walker because Walker feared he would become implicated with her if she were to be charged. Burt, who could see the solicitor did not intend to give any information which might help him, declined to discuss the matter.

Leonard Burt now knew there was not enough evidence to bring criminal proceedings against anyone and he acknowledged this in the report he was preparing on the Murfitt investigation for his Superintendent at the Yard. In the summary at the end of his 140-page report he wrote, 'A good deal of evidence is available, but it is of an exclusively circumstantial character. This, of course, is the only sort of evidence one can expect to get in a poisoning case of this nature, which, looking at the facts as I know them, seems to be the work of a woman.' His report left no doubt who he thought that woman was.

The Murfitt family, Burt noted, seemed to have accepted Bill Murfitt's murder with serenity. He wrote, 'Their attitude amounted almost to one of apathy, a rather incomprehensible outlook on their part when one considers that they knew Murfitt had suffered a foul and violent death through some agency or another. The complacency with which Mrs Murfitt apparently viewed the matter was rather troubling and accentuated the difficulties we experienced in our endeavours to eliminate her.'

He believed that the eldest son Leslie and his wife Ricky were inclined to suspect Mrs Murfitt at one time, 'They certainly were not lacking in bringing to my notice matters which affected the private life of Mr and Mrs Murfitt, and quite a lot of work was put in by these two people in their endeavours to assist me in my investigations.'

It was possible to build up a hypothetical case against Mrs Murfitt, and Mr and Mrs Browne and others, Burt wrote, but the facts did not support it. He then made it plain he knew Mrs Chandler was Murfitt's murderer.

'In her case,' Burt wrote, 'we have a number of elements present which one would expect to find in the identification of the poisoner and the construction of a prima facie case of murder.' She possessed knowledge of the layout of Quays Farm, and of the habits of the household, and she had every opportunity of learning the Murfitts' habit of taking Fynnon Salts and the position of the tin on the sideboard.

Mrs Chandler would also have had a motive in safeguarding the substantial inheritance she was to get on Walker's death. It didn't matter if the will in her favour was made in April that year or many years ago, she knew what she was to expect on Walker's death and had every reason to believe that if he came to know of her 1924 criminal conviction and full history, he might disinherit her. If she were to be convicted of stealing Mrs Waugh's fur coat in September 1937, it would provide an adequate motive for killing both Mr and Mrs Murfitt.

Burt's report continued, 'Mrs Chandler's antecedent history shows that she is a sly and cunning woman, as is evidenced by the way in which she has obtained access to the private apartments of friends' houses with the obvious intention of thieving. The effrontery shown by her in leaving the dinner table preparatory to doing so, and the commission of larcenies in the veritable presence of her hosts and other guests, discloses her as a bold person who is willing to take a risk. That she is a woman of resource is evidenced by her prompt and glib explanations when found in compromising circumstances, as she was by Mrs Murfitt.'

She was ingenious and versatile in her criminal enterprises and in ensuring freedom from detection. The way she equipped herself with alibis showed care and forethought. 'That she is indeed a wicked woman, with little or no regard for the consequences of her acts, even when it comes to the destruction of human life, is borne out by the motor-car incident, the facts of which leave little doubt that she resorted to incendiarism and the hazarding of the safety of Walker and his mother when she tampered with the car's mechanism,' Burt's wrote.

He thought her continued indisposition, the fact that she was passing through the change of life and the head injury in her childhood may well have affected her brain, bringing about mental abnormality.

When it came to possession of cyanide, Mrs Chandler had access to the poison in Walker's house, although well before Murfitt's death. One possibility was that Walker did have some cyanide left in his house up to the day of Murfitt's death, otherwise why would he have lied persistently about the presence and use of the poison in his house?

Burt then turned his thoughts to James Walker. 'I am most definitely inclined to the opinion that – to put it at its lowest – Walker knows something very material to this inquiry, but I am doubtful if we shall ever learn of it,' he wrote. 'Why has he so persistently, right from the outset, resorted to making lying statements? What is the reason for his mental confusion? Obviously the answer is that he does not want to implicate himself or Chandler.'

He added, 'The obvious collusion that has existed between Walker and Chandler throughout the inquiry is surely capable of one explanation – the connection of one or the other, or both, with the death of Murfitt. There is no other possible interpretation of their conduct… It is of interest that Walker and Chandler are the only persons who have suggested suicide.'

The detective noted that the only evidence needed to produce a prima facie case of murder against Mrs Chandler was for someone to say they saw her entering or leaving Murffitt's premises in the hours before his death. 'I think we are not likely to obtain this vital missing link unless Walker supplies it,' Burt wrote.

Venting his anger again against Mrs Chandler, Burt reported, 'In the course of our interrogation, she produced the impression that she might very well possess all the criminal qualities which have been attributed to her. In my opinion she is a hard and wicked criminal. She is an unmitigated liar who lies merely for the sake of lying.'

Had mistakes been made during the investigation which allowed the killer to escape? Burt said it might be suggested that fingerprint evidence could have helped, but unfortunately the tin of salts had been handled by several people – Mrs Murfitt, Dr Ware and the Deputy Coroner – and removed before the police ever handled it.

Burt also raised the question of why Hall Farm was not searched at the time Mrs Chandler was first told she was to face the charges of stealing or receiving Mrs Waugh's fur coat, in the hope of finding something relevant to Murfitt's death. The answer was that she was not arrested, which would have allowed a search to be made, but summonsed, which did not allow the police to take that action.

At the end of the report, Burt spoke highly of the help given by the Chief Constable in providing cars and other resources and in giving the Yard detectives a free hand in the inquiry. He praised the co-operation received from Superintendent Archie Brinkley, who conferred with them daily, often worked until the early hours and whose interest enabled an atmosphere of perfect harmony to prevail. There was praise, too for the other local officers who helped in the investigations, and for Sergeant Spooner 'who proved his sterling qualities as an able and indefatigable worker.'

Finally, on Saturday, August 27, fourteen weeks and four days after William Murfitt collapsed and died in his dining room at Quays Farm, Chief Inspector Leonard Burt wrote the paragraph that caused him most pain. 'I feel that the whole of the officers who so ably assisted in the investigation share my disappointment in not being able to satisfactorily terminate the inquiry by collating sufficient evidence to place upon trial a very dangerous poisoner.'

Two days later Superintendent Bell, to whom Burt reported at Scotland Yard, penned him a note of consolation, saying, 'It must be agreed that everything points to Mrs Chandler as being responsible for this wicked murder. She is the spiteful, cunning type of woman who would require very little motive and who would stop at nothing to get her way.' He added that their only hope was that when Mrs Chandler exhausted her money, including that which she had from the Press, she would return to Walker. 'If the latter then declines to have anything to do with her, there may be some disclosure or other development which will be to the good.'

Three weeks after he sent in his report, Burt wrote to Superintendent Bell that Mrs Chandler was now living in Cambridge and was being visited periodically by Walker. 'I am in no way surprised at this, as it was obvious at the last meeting with Walker that he did not intend to assist, in fact he was obstructive and repudiated much of the information he had previously given,' he wrote. He added, perhaps with not too much optimism, 'The only hope of solving this mystery is a quarrel between the parties – Walker may then tell us all he knows.'

It never happened. Walker sold up and moved out of Hall Farm and around the same time Mrs Chandler moved out of the Cambridge nursing home. Over the years, whenever I asked in Risby, no-one had any knowledge of where they had gone and it was only in the latter stages of writing this book that I was able to trace their subsequent lives together, as explained in the following postscript.

Mary Elizabeth Fernie Chandler, housekeeper to
James Walker

Postscript

The village

With the inquest over, Risby reverted to its former anonymity. The mystery, the scandal, the speculation, instead of being broadcast all over the nation's newspapers, was left to the pub and garden fence gossip. Preparations for war now became the main topic of conversation and within a year the first visible signs of the village's part in the defence of England came with the entry of a squad of the Middlesex Regiment, who set up sandbagged emplacements for a searchlight and a Lewis machine gun in a field off the Flempton road. The searchlight's brilliant beam sometimes reflected off the clouds and lit up the village in a way that negated the hard work put in by Moki Spalding and other ARP wardens and Special Constables in exhorting residents to 'Put that light out' to hide it from German bombers. The Army later took over a wood opposite the searchlight camp for ambulances and, with other camps and hastily-built airfields in surrounding villages, takings at the Crown and Castle and the White Horse, supplies permitting, gradually rose again after decreasing seriously since the reporters and curious visitors had departed after the murder investigations.

The lease of Quays Farm was taken up by another farmer from the Fens, Arthur Rickwood, who was as forward looking in farming methods as Bill Murfitt but quieter in personality and the farm continued to prosper. Rickwood put in a manager, Charles Smith, who moved into the farmhouse with his wife and family. From time to time during the war the garden, where Mrs Murfitt had talked with the detectives and where Rippon Charles Browne had heard of his wife's infidelity, became a scene of pleasure as village girls partnered young airmen and soldiers at dances held on the lawn to raise money for the war effort. Syd Williams stayed on as foreman until the war ended, when he achieved his ambition to be his own boss and, with his brothers Dick and Wilf, took over the lease of a smallholding on the edge of Bury St Edmunds. They managed it happily and precariously until the council took it over in the 1950s to build an industrial estate.

With James Walker gone, embarrassed by the scandal and with few friends left in the area, Hall Farm was taken over by Roger Marriage, his wife Rhoda and their young family who were always intrigued by its recent history. Their interest increased considerably when Mr Marriage, noticing one day that the Virginia creeper on the front of the house was beginning to fail, had the plant dug up to find a quantity of white powder and a tin among its roots. He informed the police and was told it was a poisonous substance but nothing further was heard of the matter.

The Murfitt family

Gertrude Murfitt went to live with her sister Kitty in Wisbech and her grand-daughter Ann joined them during holidays from boarding school. Bill Murfitt's death was never mentioned in the house but for many years, when the Murfitt family got together for funerals, there was always an unknown man present in the church and it was assumed he was a detective. While his wife Ricky continued her business career, Leslie Murfitt joined up and served with the Eighth Army. He went back into business after the war but died in the 1950s.

Young Billy Murfitt also went into the Army and on demob got involved in selling eggs in a way which may not have fully conformed with Ministry of Food regulations. One day he decided it might be a wise move to sell all his eggs, as well as the lorry he carried them in, and with the money raised he made his way to London to sign up again as a ship's engineer. He sailed all around the world and in one port, Archangel, he was thrown into prison by the Russians for a short spell on suspicion of being a spy. Back in England, he set up a second-hand furniture business in Ipswich which he later sold to buy a chicken farm. When we met he was in his late 80s and living in Bedfordshire.

The Brownes continued to farm in Fornham All Saints, although it was plain to Elaine Browne's friends that the strain of the inquest and its revelations had affected her health. She died in 1948 and her husband in 1972.

The policemen

Chief Inspector Leonard Burt returned to London, his career undimmed by his failure to bring Bill Murfitt's poisoner to justice. He was promoted Chief Superintendent CID at the Yard and in 1940 he was seconded to MI5. As a Lieutenant-Colonel in the Intelligence Corps he formed a team specialising in anti-sabotage and anti-espionage and his deputy was Captain Reginald Spooner. Their headquarters was a commandeered cell in Wormwood Scrubs prison in West London, which led to ribald comments from their former colleagues in the Met. At the end of the war they again worked together, in Europe tracing 20 traitors including William Joyce – better known as Lord Haw Haw – and John Amery. Spooner, then a major, was also Burt's assistant when they arrested the atom spy Nunn May.

Burt returned to Scotland Yard in 1946 to become Commander in Charge of the Special Branch. He arrested another spy, Klaus Fuchs, in 1949 and travelled the world with the Royal Family, responsible for their safety. He retired in 1958 and wrote his autobiography, in which the Murfitt case merited only one paragraph. In it, referring to insoluble murders, he wrote, 'Not all are really without solution so much as without evidence of sufficient weight to convince a jury.' But he may well have had Fernie Chandler in mind when he wrote elsewhere in the book, 'Nobody may look more innocent than a guilty person – the demure yet deceptive lady is a case in point.' Later, in comparing women criminals with men criminals, he commented, 'In my experience they are certainly more accomplished and convincing liars.' Burt died in 1983 aged 91.

Reg Spooner was demobilised from the Intelligence Corps in 1946 and, always a workaholic, went back to the Yard the same day. Soon afterwards he was in the headlines again as the man who sent Neville Heath to the gallows for the horrific torture and murder of an actress named Margery Gardner. In 1954 he was put in charge of the then ailing Flying Squad, known in the Cockney rhyming slang which he loved to use as the Sweeney, or in full Sweeney Todd, which was later to have its own fame in the TV series. The Flying Squad improved beyond all measure and he became a national celebrity, earning praise from the newspapers for being 'ace detective,' 'master crime-buster' and 'one of the greatest investigators ever known at Scotland Yard.' His life of hard work, hard drinking and heavy smoking eventually caught up with him and he died from lung cancer in 1963, aged 60 and still in The Job. A thousand policemen attended his funeral.

A biography of Reg Spooner published in 1966, entitled The Great Detective, devoted a chapter to the Murfitt case. It records how in 1938 he wrote home to his wife Myra just before the Murfitt inquest that he and Burt were practically certain who was responsible for the murder. 'We just cannot get that little bit of evidence to prove it,' he wrote. 'We are still living in hopes, but the odds are 1,000 to one against getting it and we cannot do anything without it.' He would tell colleagues of the fantastic risks the murderer took in putting cyanide in Murfitt's Fynnon Salts and when asked why that person had not been spotted at the time replied, 'It was just poisoner's luck.'

In December 1938 the West Suffolk Chief Constable Captain Colin Robertson was recalled to his old regiment as the build-up to war continued and Archibald Brinkley took over the force until he returned in 1940. Robertson retired in bad health in 1945.

The Coroner

Thomas Wilson carried on his public duties to a late age and he was still Coroner when he died in 1972 at the age of 89. He was the last of the franchised coroners and within two years of his death, under local government re-organisation, the appointments were then made by the county council, partly to stop any suggestion of nepotism when the post was passed down among families. This did not stop his nephew, Bill Walrond, later being appointed by the council to the same position.

Wilson's handling of the Murfitt inquest was questioned soon after the hearing in an article in the London Evening Standard which said he had 'filled the role of a judge in a criminal trial' in his summing up by guiding the jury to consider motives and opportunity for the farmer's death in relation to four of the witnesses. 'Now, none of these witnesses was in court as an accused person, against none of them had the police found any evidence warranting arrest and trial. Yet against each of them the coroner pointed the finger of presumptive guilt,' the article said, adding, 'Slung mud sticks.'

The article did not impugn Wilson's impartiality or criticise 'his sense of judicial propriety.' It went on, 'As from a Judge of Assize, his summing up was fair and lucid. The point is that it never should have had such scope.' The article went on to call for a new Parliamentary Act to 'codify inquest practice.' It took more than forty years after for the Coroners' Rules to be changed by law and if the Murfitt inquest were to be held today the jury would only be able to bring a verdict of unlawful killing and could not be asked to name the culprit.

The Laing-Walkers

After the scandal had subsided James Laing Walker achieved the quiet life he desired by a simple but effective hyphenated change of name, becoming Mr Laing-Walker. This move, which changed the order of his name in any alphabetical registers and lists, made it difficult to trace his movements for the purpose of this book. Mrs Chandler changed her name to Fernie May Elizabeth Laing-Walker and they moved to Horley in Surrey, where during the war they ran the Cambridge Hotel – the name perhaps a reference to the city where she sought refuge from her problems in 1938.

The hotel was a success and they eventually retired to live by the sea at St Leonards, Sussex, where James Laing-Walker died in 1971 at the age of 91. Fernie was his sole executrix and beneficiary to his net estate of nearly £15,000. She continued to live in their house on a new development in Gillsmans Park, troubled only by regular burglars and failing sight. As her health deteriorated a district nurse, Margaret Turner, was called in to attend her and they became good friends. She never spoke much about her past but did mention her life in India. Mrs Turner thought she was given to bringing a little fantasy into her history when she mentioned she had Royal connections, especially when she said she had made Princess Margaret's wedding cake and been invited to a garden party at Buckingham Palace where, she claimed, the Queen Mother took her on one side and they talked of their early days in Scotland. She also said she had driven ambulances in France in World War I – questionable since she would have been only 17 in 1914.

Mrs Turner knew Fernie Laing-Walker as a lively lady right to the end of her life, cooking, making jams and being keen and knowledgeable on gardening. She did well with her investments and bought an ambulance for the local charity for the blind which had her name painted on the side. She died of cancer in 1994 at the age of 97 and when her house was being cleared Mrs Turner bought a memento of her friend, an embroidered picture of a young girl. She did not know that the signature on the back, Minnie R Townsend, was that of James Walker's first wife. Fernie Laing-Walker, of humble beginnings, left net estate of £695,173, making legacies to Mrs Turner and a niece in Scotland, with a trust fund paying a lifetime interest to a friend the Laing-Walkers made when they ran the hotel. The will instructed that this interest should later pass to a niece and on her death the capital and interest of the fund should pass to the Royal National Lifeboat Institution. Fifty six years after William Murfitt died of cyanide poisoning, and after a life of adventure, mystery, deception and no little fantasy, the woman the two Scotland Yard detectives knew murdered him died respected in her community, where her criminal past was unknown and leaving a fortune which will eventually benefit a worthy charity.

This book

When I joined the Bury Free Press as a junior reporter in 1949 I asked the other reporters if they knew anything of Murfitt's murder, but a war had intervened and no-one did. Frank Williams, still running the Bury St Edmunds office for the East Anglian Daily Times, did remember but he said it was a mystery that would never be solved. He also quite rightly pointed out that any story at that time which might point the finger of accusation towards anyone still living could have legal and costly consequences.

In the 1950s, in the early hours of one morning when things were quiet in the newsroom of the Daily Mirror, I sent to the editorial library for cuttings on the murder. As I read the file I realised that the information I had gained from the Bury Free Press files barely skimmed the surface of the drama at the time. I wrote to Leonard Burt soon after he retired to ask if I could interview him about his investigation in Risby. I received a quick but curt reply that he remembered very little about it and there would be no point in our meeting. After a career filled with so many successes it was obvious that he did not want to dredge up one of his rare failures. Also, at that time Mrs Chandler and Walker were still alive and any mention of them as being responsible for the murder would have been legally dangerous.

On frequent visits back to Risby I tried to draw out more information from my father, but although he repeated the anecdotes he had told me before he obviously did not have any more background knowledge than anyone else in the village. Bearing in mind the seriousness of the case, he always treated the death of his former boss fairly light-heartedly, taking delight in producing a discoloured dessert spoon with Murfitt's name engraved on the handle and telling any visitor to our house that it was the spoon that poisoned William Murfitt. He would never be drawn on whom he suspected of the murder. 'Wouldn't you just like to know,' he would say with a devilish grin and I told him yes I would, but I didn't believe he or anyone else in the village knew.

Thirty seven years after I left Bury St Edmunds I returned to edit the Bury Free Press for the last eight happy years before retirement and we found a house in Risby, halfway between Quays Farm and Hall Farm. But I was still too busy to contemplate a book.

Just before I retired in 1997 I wrote a feature about the murder in the Bury Free Press to help publicise a local history exhibition in the village, asking if anyone had any information which might lead to solving the mystery. This excited the attention of other media, including the Daily Mail which sent one of their star writers, Paul Harris, to write a feature on the almost-forgotten case. He discovered the then owners of Quays Farm, Mick and Jane McNeil, had found a medicine bottle while doing repairs and often wondered if it was the one that had contained the killer cyanide. But it was not a promising clue, and we were no nearer to finding the poisoner. But the interest the features caused made me decide that at last the case must be researched and the book written.

I asked Scotland Yard if they could help with any information and learned that the Murfitt file, which had been locked away since 1938, had been passed to the Public Records Office in 1994, the year Mrs Chandler died, and was now in the public domain, although no-one had accessed it.

I had letters published in newspapers throughout East Anglia asking for information, including the whereabouts of the Murfitt family. Through one of these published in the Kings Lynn News and Advertiser I came into contact with Bill Knowles, who as well as being a long-serving coroner for that part of Norfolk was also Murfitt's great nephew. He, in turn, put me in touch with Ann Heading, who as Leslie Murfitt's little daughter had been called from her prep school classroom to be asked if she knew her grandfather took health salts every morning when she visited her grandparents at Risby.

It transpired that, following publication of the Daily Mail's feature on the case, Bill and Ann had visited Risby and been shown round Quays Farm, now a house separate from the farm, by the McNeil's. Ann had also taken her uncle Billy Murfitt, then well into his eighties and living in Bedfordshire, to revisit the house where he had built his beloved Flying Flea and where he had returned in sadness from his ship in the Mediterranean after receiving the radio message about his father's death. Ann arranged for me to meet Billy at a Sunday lunch at her home near Huntingdon and he still had clear memories of his father's death and how it had affected the family at the time.

After tracing surviving members of the Waugh family in New-market, I travelled to Dorset to meet Peggy Otter, daughter of Dawson and Edith Waugh, now in her 90s but still with a sharp recollection of the fur coat case. She told me the story of how her mother had recognised the hidden talent of the little yearling at the Doncaster sales and had taken it through its successful racing career and sold it, spending some of the proceeds on the coat which Fernie Chandler was eventually accused of stealing. Even after all this time, Mrs Otter was convinced that her uncle, James Walker, had known Mrs Chandler before she ever appeared in Risby and that the pair had poisoned her Aunt Minnie so that they could later set up home together. She said her mother had been of the same opinion but had balked at the idea of her sister being dug up from her grave in Risby churchyard for tests to be carried out.

Through Vince Matthews, who had built up a family tree of the Townsend family from which Minnie Walker came, I learned how Walker had changed his surname to Laing-Walker and had given that name to Fernie Chandler on their marriage. I was then able, through the excellent service provided by Traceline, a department of the Office for National Statistics, to follow their trail to the hotel in Horley, Surrey, and to their eventual retirement in Sussex.

Edna Kydd, widow of Murfitt's chauffeur Ted and still living at that time in Risby, gave me her memories of the time and their son Ian contributed the story of Murfitt's bizarre windbreaking habits as Ted drove his boss and his lady friends in the black Buick. John Ashton, in his 90s and still living in Bury St Edmunds, told me how his family law firm had been closely involved in all the legal proceedings affecting the case and how, as a young solicitor, he had withdrawn from one of the hearings because he knew Mrs Chandler personally through playing badminton with her. Clem Fuller, also in his 90s, told me how, as West Suffolk's first detective, he had missed out on the big investigation by being away on a course, although he was able to fill in valuable background about how the local police force operated at the time. Bill Walrond, retired as Coroner for Bury St Edmunds, checked details for me about his uncle Thomas Wilson.

All this built up for me a fascinating and detailed picture of how a Suffolk village had its quiet life shattered by the violence of murder and how it was thrust unwillingly into the spotlight of a major police investigation and the consequent sensational publicity in that summer of 1938. It also enabled me, more than 60 years after he was poisoned, to name Mary Elizabeth Fernie Chandler as William Murfitt's murderer.

OTHER THOROGOOD TITLES

A TASTE OF WARTIME BRITAIN

Edited by Nicholas Webley
£9.99 paperback, published in 2003

A vivid and evocative collection of eye-witness accounts, diaries, reportage and scraps of memory from people who lived through the dark days of World War II. Lavishly illustrated with many newspaper pictures and personal photos, the book shows what life was like for millions of ordinary people throughout the war – men, women, children, soldiers and civilians. It brilliantly captures the sights, the smells and sounds and the voices of a country at war.

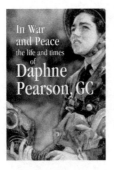

IN WAR AND PEACE – THE LIFE AND TIMES OF DAPHNE PEARSON GC

An autobiography • £17.99 cased, published in 2002

Daphne Pearson, born in 1911, was the first woman to be given the George Cross, it was awarded for acts of courage in circumstances of extreme danger. This is the inspiring story of a very courageous and remarkable woman.

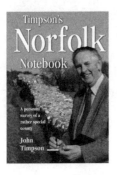

TIMPSON'S NORFOLK NOTEBOOK

John Timpson
£9.99 paperback, published in 2002

A collection of renowned writer and broadcaster John Timpson's best writing about Norfolk, its ancient and subtle landscape, places with strange tales to tell, remarkable and eccentric people and old legends and traditions.

A LIFE OF JOHN HAMPDEN – THE PATRIOT

John Adair

£12.99 paperback, published in 2003

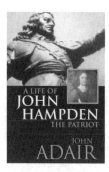

John Hampden, statesman and soldier, was a cousin to Oliver Cromwell and, had he not met an untimely death at the Battle of Chalgrove during the Civil World War in 1643, he might well have achieved similar fame in English history, both as a soldier and parliamentarian. This classic study of a great man has been out of print for some years and is now published in paperback for the first time.

JELLIED EELS AND ZEPPELINS

Sue Taylor

£8.99 paperback, published in 2003

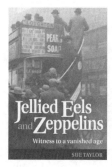

As every year goes by, the number of people able to give a first hand account of day-to-day life in the early part of the last century naturally diminishes. The small but telling detail disappears. Ethel May Elvin was born in 1906; she recalls her father's account of standing sentry at Queen Victoria's funeral, the privations and small pleasures of a working class Edwardian childhood, growing up through the First World War and surviving the Second. Anyone intrigued by the small events of history, how the majority actually lived day-to-day, will find this a unique and fascinating book.

IN SEARCH OF SECRET SUFFOLK

Robert Leader

£9.99 paperback, published in 2004

A book of discovery which explores the heritage and landscape of Suffolk. Uniquely, it follows the course of each of Suffolk's rivers and looks at the towns, villages, stately homes and churches that grew up in their valleys. Robert Leader also charts the medieval history and tradition of the once great abbeys, castles and guildhalls.

CONFESSIONS OF A COUNTRY BOY

Keith Skipper
£8.99 paperback, published in 2002

Memories of a Norfolk childhood fifty years ago: this is broadcaster and humorist Keith Skipper in his richest vein, sharp and witty, occasionally disrespectful, always affectionate. As he says himself 'Distance may lend enchantment, but my country childhood has inspired much more than rampant nostalgia. I relish every chance to extol the virtues of a golden age when... life was quieter, slower, simpler...'

'He delights our days and does so much for Norfolk.'
Malcolm Bradbury

BETTY'S WARTIME DIARY – 1939-1945

Edited by Nicholas Webley
£9.99 paperback, published in 2002

The Second World War diary of a Norfolk seamstress. Here, the great events of those years are viewed from the country: privation relieved by poaching, upheaval as thousands of bright young US servicemen 'invade' East Anglia, quiet heroes and small-time rural villains. Funny, touching and unaffectedly vivid.

'Makes unique reading... I am finding it fascinating.'
David Croft, co-writer and producer of BBC's hit comedy series 'Dad's Army'